ELIZABETH BARRETT BROWNING

✳

LONGMANS, GREEN AND CO.
55 FIFTH AVENUE, NEW YORK
221 EAST 20TH STREET, CHICAGO
TREMONT TEMPLE, BOSTON
128 UNIVERSITY AVENUE, TORONTO

LONGMANS, GREEN AND CO. LTD.
39 PATERNOSTER ROW, E C 4, LONDON
53 NICOL ROAD, BOMBAY
6 OLD COURT HOUSE STREET, CALCUTTA
167 MOUNT ROAD, MADRAS

ELIZABETH BARRETT BROWNING

ELIZABETH BARRETT BROWNING

BY

LOUISE SCHUTZ BOAS

LONGMANS, GREEN AND CO.
LONDON · NEW YORK · TORONTO
1930

BOAS
ELIZABETH BARRETT BROWNING

COPYRIGHT · 1930
BY LOUISE SCHUTZ BOAS

FIRST EDITION

PRINTED IN THE UNITED STATES OF AMERICA

To

ANNE C. E. ALLINSON

ACKNOWLEDGMENTS

PERMISSION has kindly been granted by Harper & Brothers to quote from *Letters of Robert Browning and Elizabeth Barrett, 1845-1846;* and by The Macmillan Company to quote from *The Letters of Elizabeth Barrett Browning*.

LIST OF ILLUSTRATIONS

O lyric Love, half angel and half bird,
And all a wonder and a wild desire, —
Boldest of hearts that ever braved the sun,
Took sanctuary within the holier blue,
And sang a kindred soul out to his face, —
Yet human at the red-ripe of the heart —
When the first summons from the darkling earth
Reached thee amid thy chambers, blanched their blue,
And bared them of the glory — to drop down,
To toil for man, to suffer or to die, —
This is the same voice: can thy soul know change?
Hail then, and hearken from the realms of help!
Never may I commence my song, my due
To God who best taught song by gift of thee,
Except with bent head and beseeching hand —
That still, despite the distance and the dark,
What was, again may be; some interchange
Of grace, some splendor once thy very thought,
Some benediction anciently thy smile:
— Never conclude, but raising hand and head
Thither where eyes, that cannot reach, yet yearn
For all hope, all sustainment, all reward,
Their utmost up and on, — so blessing back
In those thy realms of help, that heaven thy home,
Some whiteness which, I judge, thy face makes proud,
Some wanness where, I think, thy foot may fall!

ROBERT BROWNING

CHAPTER I

As green as any privet-hedge a bird
Might choose to build in

was the tower room where the child Elizabeth Barrett
sat and poetized. Delicately poised on the window-seat
with the sun dimly penetrating the stained glass panes,
the little poet composed her first great works. The honey-
suckle vines embraced the casement, the green curtains
tempered the colored lights that danced on green carpet
and green-draped bed, and the dreamy child with curls
falling over her serious face leaned against the green wall
as she guided her pencil over a tiny slip of paper. Thus
early was the poet enshrined; thus early was she set apart
and taught to think of herself as an interesting individual.

Hope End, her father's estate, was sufficiently lordly for
a setting. It lay in a small valley surrounded by hills of
moderate eminence; and the house was set behind stiffly
ornamented ponds. The Deer Park on the mounds was
carefully wooded; and there had been a conscious attempt
to create "scenery." The house itself was startling; instead of a weathered English house blending with its
surroundings, there rose up an immense Alladin's palace,
an Arabian Nights' dream of domes and turrets crowned
with metal spires and crescents, stained glass windows,
grills, and fretwork balconies.

The Hope End dwelling was the romance of a young man whose early childhood had been spent in Jamaica. Edward Barrett Moulton (who later at his grandfather's bequest became Edward Barrett Moulton-Barrett) had come to England at his father's death, thoroughly imbued with autocratic ideas. His indulgent mother was prompt to remove him from Harrow at his complaint of savage punishment for having burned an older boy's toast. His resentment was far keener than that of one bred in English traditions which taught the sons of gentlemen to endure stoically the abuse of other gentlemen's sons; he could not brook being treated as he would have treated a black slave. The brutality of English schoolboys too much parallelled that of Jamaican slave-owners. His protests were sufficiently vigorous to cause his withdrawal and the expulsion of the lad who had tyrannized over him. His great wealth made him important as he well realized; and his pompous name sounded to him noble, if not regal.

Cambridge failed to tame him. Before he was twenty he was through with schooling and had embarked upon full adult life, marrying a gentle lady whose superior age flattered his love of authority. She was not consulted about the building of the Turkish mansion; she was told when to betake herself and her two children — Elizabeth, born in March 1806, now three years old, and Edward two years younger — to the new home.

Mrs. Barrett, naturally a sweet, gentle, submissive creature, lived for nearly twenty years in the seclusion of Hope End unprotected from the thunder of her husband's anger. Somewhat soured by constant yielding to her tyrant she crept unresisting through the monotonous decades, bearing patiently four daughters and eight sons. One daughter died in infancy; the remaining eleven children lived to mourn her dutifully when in 1828 she passed out of her colorless existence. Alive or dead she meant little to them. The sentimental Elizabeth, whom the disappearance of a pet dog prostrated, bore her loss without great emotion; and in later years made scarce more than conventionally correct allusions to her, and these few.

The father, however, was a positive person ruling his small kingdom with pomp and regal severity. He was the all-wise patriarch — and here his comparative youth betrayed him into unwarranted dignity — who knew best both when his children were young and when they were adult. Their happiness and well-being, he felt, depended entirely upon him; it was his duty to rule them for their good by his divine right of parenthood. It must be remembered that he was actually a slave-owner and that his earliest years had been spent in Jamaica with slaves serving him. In England he did not have his black slaves about him; but at Hope End remote from village and neighbors he had his own little colony, his wife and children who soon learned to obey the crack of his verbal whip.

His affection for his children was that of a proprietor for his possessions. "After using one's children as one's chattels for a time," wrote Elizabeth years later of her father, "the children drop lower and lower toward the level of the chattels, and the duties of human sympathy to them become difficult in proportion. And . . . love . . . he does not understand, any more than he understands Chaldee, respecting it less of course." When she was younger, however, she believed that he loved her, and she always believed that she loved him. Filial devotion was a Victorian fundamental; never did the numerous Barretts admit that they were not devoted to their father. They honestly thought that they "revered" him; and he was credulous that they did. Since their very existence, their food and shelter, depended upon his goodwill, even after they became adult, they were necessarily obedient.

But their obedience was that of chattels. As children they developed the tactics of slaves, their unusually keen intelligence teaching them how best to outwit their master by seeming submission. In his presence they were grateful for kindness, fearful of anger, careful of propitiatory rites. In his absence they, as children, and later as adults, were adept in ignoring his laws and in indulging in forbidden activities. The loyalty of slave to slave prevented any one of them from reporting the sins of others; and there were always one's own pecadilloes to conceal. The chief aim of their morality rapidly became to keep father from knowing. They developed the habit of fawning and of double dealing. When he thundered, all prostrated themselves; and thunder, being unpleasant, was by any means to be avoided. If he were ignorant of causes for thunder, a stretch of fair weather might reasonably be expected.

Elizabeth was by far the most skilful of the family both in averting wrath and in acquiring merit. She soon learned to meet a frown with a gay smile and a flourish of a diminutive slip of paper. "See my poem, papa!" she would cry, offering for his perusal a couplet of filial reverence. Barrett was charmed with his precocious daughter's talent. He encouraged her to write more and more. He gave his little jewel a properly sentimental setting; hence the green room whither he liked to conduct his friends to see the child, her curls sweeping her flushed face as she struggled with rhymes or listened intently to the music of Pope's *Homer,* reading on oblivious to the world about her. Poetry to her was more than amusement; it was a passion. To her the name of poet was royal. Poets were "the only truth-tellers left to God," the true teachers of men. Romance and religion she found in poetry. Her devotion was genuine, as was also her setting up as a poet, though she was undoubtedly influenced by her father's idea of her, falling readily into the groove he made for her.

And with a child's sense of the dramatic she soon acted the part more and more thoroughly. It did not become a devotee of the Muses to be robust and hoydenish; rather should she seem dreamy and delicate. She could not at once divorce herself from habits of outdoor play especially as Edward, the beloved "Bro," close in heart as in age, dearest to her of all her family, clamored for his companion in rides and excursions. She still helped him catch pretty little field-mice to train as pets, and joined in many an unlawful exploit.

Nor was her garden neglected. While her brothers and sisters cultivated the ordinary stars and crescents, circles and diamonds for their plots, Elizabeth made what seemed to her a human figure which, true to Homer, she called Hector. Lovingly she planted his blue eyes, his ruddy cheeks, his silver armor; and reverently she raked and hoed him. But now she frequently escaped from her playmates to take lonely walks about the estate, penetrating the conveniently near woods where she would find fairy bowers and romantically deserted gardens.

More and more she tended to live an inward life, cultivating her dreams more carefully than her garden; and trying to live up to her father's and her own conception of herself as a poet. She would wake early and sit by the window genuinely thrilled at the coming of dawn. Sometimes she would stir up her courage to steal through the sleeping house and glide through the garden in the dim light before the sun had come. Such thrills, however, were not for frequent repetition; one couldn't be quite sure about ghosts; and on the whole it was pleasanter to dream of oneself in the dim quiet among the flowers than actually to be there. One who shuddered over the bats which in summer nights flew in and out of the turret chamber was not over ready for daring deeds. And as she grew older Elizabeth's attention was more and more withdrawn from garden and sports to the world of books.

Her father encouraged her constantly; it pleased him to have a scholar in the family, all the more because he was himself no scholar. And so Elizabeth was given Homer to read (in Pope's version) not many years before the child Robert Browning, whose "father was a scholar and knew Greek," had the tale unfolded to him with chairs and tables piled up for Troy town, Robert himself for Priam, his pony for Achilles, and the cat for Helen. Elizabeth's father's instruction was full as vivid though more terrifying. He would put Elizabeth on the mantel, bidding her "Stand up straight like a hero !" and keeping her there until the imaginative child felt the walls "growing alive behind [her] and extending two bony hands to push [her] down that frightful precipice to the rug, where the dog lay — dear old Havannah — where he and [she] were likely to be dashed to pieces together and mix [their] uncanonized bones."

She did not communicate her terror to a father who thought such treatment encouraging to his daughter's poetical development. Certainly, in spite of his methods, he succeeded, and at eight the child plunged boldly into authorship. No lover of physical heights, she scribbled away sitting firmly on the floor or perching on the arm of a large chair. Odes and epics flowed from her pencil and moral verses were not slow to follow. Filial piety was pleasanter versified than observed. She could "write of virtue with a large 'V' " while her brothers and sisters were made to practice it; she could write "O Muse with a harp" while they had to pound scales on a piano.

> And so, like most young poets, in a flush
> Of individual life I poured myself
> Along the veins of others, and achieved
> Mere lifeless imitations of live verse,

and

Wrote false poems . . . and thought them true
Because myself was true in writing them.

These juvenilia were kept in "little clasped books" which the child would kiss and put away tenderly, loving them because she had been happy with them, transferring her joy in creative writing to the books as symbols. Whenever she went visiting, these books accompanied her; or if it were not possible to take them all, as they increased in number, then she would give them turns to profit by the change of air. For her they had personalities as definite as those of the books she loved to read.

And though her father was less interested in poetry than in having a poet in the family, Elizabeth was truly sprinkled with fairy dust. At nine she wrote an epic; at ten "various tragedies, French and English," among them a tragedy in French hexameters on the subject of Regulus, concocted as the child crouched in an imaginary house under the massive sideboard in the dining-room. These ambitious tragedies the older Barrett children acted in the nursery to their own satisfaction and that of their father who somewhat unbent on these occasions and permitted much latitude of costume and antic.

Edward, the oldest boy, was now ready for a tutor. Edward — usually called "Bro" — and Elizabeth, who throughout life was seldom called by anything but the name he gave her, "Ba," the first syllable of baby, were such devoted companions that their threatened separation in the schoolroom was high tragedy. Elizabeth's deep devotion to Greece via Pope led the two to draw up a petition to their father that she be permitted to share the tutor's instruction. Mr. Barrett had no aversion to the learned female; besides there was no danger that Elizabeth would be led astray while he was at hand to guide her. She plunged headlong into Greek, treating paradigms with airy lightness, somehow wresting the meaning from her text. She turned aside to gain enough mastery over Latin to help her with Greek; Roman learning, however, held small charm for her. Exact scholarship was never to her mind. Her brother with university before him had to master grammar and struggle with the essentials. Elizabeth preferred to "guess the meaning of unknown words instead of looking into the dictionary" with the same eager impatience with which she tore open letters and packages never stopping to untie a string. *"Testa lunga," headlong,* the Italian master called her justly. But she was not tied down to university requirements; she could let her learning count for pleasure. Her grandmother protested: "I would rather see Elizabeth's hemming more carefully finished off than hear of all this Greek !"

The child was completely drunk with the wine of Parnassus. The Olympian deities ruled her universe more truly than her tyrannical father. Gods and goddesses found themselves in her theology strangely reconciled with Christ. With her "pinafore full of little sticks (and a match from the housemaid's cupboard)" she sallied forth to "sacrifice to the blue-eyed Minerva," who was her favorite goddess because, forsooth, "she cared for Athens" ! Mr. Barrett was not aware of these pagan rites. Throughout his life he believed his children incapable of doing without his knowledge and consent anything of which he would disapprove. He was a religious man, sufficiently concerned with the souls of others to lead religious meetings for workingmen in the neighboring town. He was ignorant of his pet's paganized Christianity based so firmly upon her belief in the gods of Olympus that when later she came to doubt them she doubted God Himself, ending her nightly prayers with a plea culled from a book not recommended by her father: "O God, if there be a God, save my soul if I have a soul."

Mr. Barrett's discipline was built, it would seem, on a system of Don't ! "Don't read Gibbon's History —" he said, "it's not a proper book. Don't read *Tom Jones*— and none of the books on this side, mind !" He knew his children dared not disobey; hence when he came into the library to find Elizabeth on the sofa absorbed in a book, one glance at the forbidden shelves satisfied him. Years later she herself wrote: "So I was very obedient and never touched the books on *that* side, and only read instead Tom Paine's *Age of Reason,* and Voltaire's *Philosophical Dictionary,* and Hume's *Essay,* and Werther, and Rousseau, and Mary Wollstonecraft — books which I was never suspected of looking towards and which were not on *that* side certainly, but which did as well."

However, long before the child's omnivorous reading led her into these paths she had her "fits of Pope, and Byron, and Coleridge, and read Greek as hard under the trees as some of your Oxonians in the Bodleian; gathered visions from Plato and the dramatists, and ate and drank Greek." So strongly was she attracted to Greece, to

Byron, and to romance, so truly was she feminine that she "used to think seriously of dressing up like a boy and running away to be Lord Byron's page."

Instead she remained quietly at Hope End devouring romantic novels and poems until the characters became as real to her as the Greek heroes of her translations and rhymes. Released from the regular routine of the school-room, she was free to follow her own fancy, studying the ancients with the tutor and the moderns with herself. Such a schedule avoided mathematics with its exact demands. She wrote naïvely: "I believe there are people who will tell you in a moment what three times six is without 'doing it' on their fingers"; she was happier wresting music from pages of Greek.

When she and her favorite brother had evaded their father's laws and the importunities of the multitude of smaller children, there was little to distract them from their pursuits. In the seclusion of Hope End, save for a very few neighbors, their days and months and years passed without social intercourse. Visiting relatives came and went, none very exacting on the children's time except one uncle whose pride in Elizabeth was almost as great as her father's. Indeed he rather hurt the child's feelings by assuring her that he was even more interested in her and more fond of her. Bred as she was to look up to her father as the household deity she could not consciously admit any lesser gods. Nevertheless, her natural sweetness responded to her uncle's affection; and to him many years later she owed her release from the Barrett prison. Thanks to his generosity in willing to her a livable income she alone of the children was financially independent.

In her childhood, however, she did not feel her home a prison. The Barrett children were a merry crew, good-natured, devoted to one another, fond of play, and apparently quite free from inherited idiosyncrasy. There were enough of them for the organized sports dear to English hearts, especially as their father was, in his gentler moods, always ready to enter into a game of cricket with his boys. The children managed long hours away from parental supervision, especially Edward and Elizabeth. And the beauty of lawns and woods and gardens, the lovely detail of trees and flowers, moonlit ponds, blossoming shrubs and hedges made for the sensitive child a joyous circle of seasons. Surrounded by loveliness, with daily life made easy by her father's great wealth, Elizabeth happily followed her own bent, appreciative of the world of nature, alive to the world of mind.

Unlike many a child poet she had no need to conceal her rhyming efforts; she could lay them at the paternal altar sure of appreciation and praise. So much did her poetizing please her father and gratify his pride that, when at thirteen she had completed her grand epic, the *Battle of Marathon,* Mr. Barrett carried it to a printer and had fifty copies made to be distributed among relatives and friends. The child's joy then was as great as her mortification years later when the poem would persist in rising to plague the famous poetess. But at thirteen it was intoxicating to view her own Popean couplets on pages fair as any of his own. And it was not distressing as she read

THE

BATTLE OF MARATHON.

A POEM.

--------------------------- " Behold
What care employs me now, my vows I pay
To the sweet Muses, teachers of my youth !"
AKENSIDE.

" Ancient of days ! August Athena ! Where,
Where are thy men of might, thy grand in soul?
Gone—glimmering through the dream of things that were.
First in the race that led to glory's goal,
They won, and past away.' BYRON.

BY E. B. BARRETT.

𝕷𝖔𝖓𝖉𝖔𝖓:

PRINTED FOR W. LINDSELL, 87, WIMPOLE-
STREET, CAVENDISH-SQUARE.

1820.

to find "Persia's haughty King," "Asia's powerful Prince,"
"Vulcan's artful spouse," "Cytherea's heart," "Æneas'
wrongs," "unconquered Greece," "Mighty Jove,"
"Athena's brazen gate," "Miltiades' stern fate," "wrath
divine," "Ilium prostrate," and "thunder thro' the skies":
all the learned allusions and stock phrases of heroic couplet and Anglicized mythology.

Seven years later in 1826 her first volume of verse was
offered to the public, taking its title from the didactic
poem *An Essay on Mind*. This was a pretentious effort full of elided e's—pow'r, flow'r, whisper'd, ador'd,
hush'd,— apostrophes to

> Man ! Man ! thou poor antithesis of power !
> Child of all time !   Yet creature of an hour !
> By turns, camelion of a thousand forms,
> The lord of empires, and the food of worms !

grandiloquent questions: "Where stands the Syra-
cusan?"; references to Dryden, Æsop, Newton, Thucy-
dides, Campbell, Bentley, Shakespeare, Klopstock, Kepler,
Gibbon, "Byron, the Mont Blanc of intellect," Tom
Paine, Dante, Tully, and Plato; with a goodly sprinkling
of Time's and Truth's, Fancy's, Philosophy's, and
Science's.

Nevertheless, however perturbed Elizabeth was to have
it resurrected in later years, it showed much talent — an
active if still imitative intellect, and an ability to handle
the herioc couplet if not with distinction at least not with
disgrace. Moreover, it displayed an astonishingly wide acquaintance with the history and vocabulary of thought

and learning, the result of long studious hours which natural inclination and months of invalidism had promoted.

When she was fifteen, Elizabeth had her first serious illness which she herself in after years attributed to congestion of the lungs with a threat of tuberculosis. Popular rumor assigned it to an injury of the spine caused by a fall from horseback; but what injury there was to the spine was never great, and was caused by a strain when the impatient girl, unwilling to wait for help, attempted to tighten the girth of her pony's saddle. The respiratory trouble was more serious, persisting at intervals throughout her life.

This illness, though temporary, started Elizabeth's lifelong rôle as a fainting female. The tradition of her delicate health was at this time firmly established. And as this gave her more freedom to follow her studious tastes, ill health brought more privileges than it took away. At this dreamy stage of adolescence it was not unpleasant to be treated tenderly, to be freed from undesired activities, to be a centre of interest. Her health was a matter of concern to herself, her family, and her friends; for years to come she rarely received or composed a letter without a query or report on the state of her health.

In time she recovered sufficiently to leave her room and to enjoy outdoors in an approved ladylike fashion. Partly as a compensation to her for her loss of health her father secured an introduction for her to Hugh Stuart Boyd, the blind scholar who lived not far from Hope End. For years Elizabeth studied with him, reading aloud to him in her pleasant, somewhat shrill voice. They were equally devoted to Greek. Boyd turned her attention to the Greek Christian poets, imparting to her his enthusiasm. She was no meek pupil, merely echoing her master's praises; again and again she would stoutly defend her own interpretation. The inequality of their ages mattered little to these two; their common love of Greek led them into a friendship that lasted until Boyd's death a quarter of a century later, a friendship marked by many a gift of rare Cyprus wine to her and many a poem to him.

The current of Elizabeth's life was not disturbed until she was twenty-six when heavy reverses made it necessary for Mr. Barrett to reduce their luxurious manner of living. Mrs. Barrett's death four years earlier had not seriously disturbed the household; Elizabeth's sister Henrietta had readily undertaken what supervision was necessary. But now abrupt change was in the air. Hope End was to be sold. Mr. Barrett bade his children prepare for immediate departure. Up to the very moment of leaving, their life went on as usual except that Mr. Barrett, while brooking no questions, was rather more friendly with his children, on their last night at Hope End joining the boys in a game of cricket. He neither showed nor permitted them to show any emotion over separation from the only home they had known.

And now, at twenty-six, Elizabeth, with two sisters and six brothers, set out to see something of the world. The journey to Sidmouth, where a furnished house had been rented, took two days with a stop overnight at Bath. To the sheltered Barretts travelling was a venture into the unknown. They had never before seen the sea; at Sidmouth they were settled a hundred and fifty yards from it. Their house was "one which the Grand Duchess Helena had, not at all *grand,* but extremely comfortable and cheerful, with a splendid sea view in front, and pleasant green hills and trees behind." Moreover, being further south, Sidmouth offered flowers and shrubs of ranker growth than Hope End. To Mr. Barrett the change from opulence to mere wealth was tragic. To Elizabeth, with her cheerful nature, the present by its very contrast to the past was stimulating. The four windows of the drawing-room looked directly out upon the sea; and to her the sea was new and strange and marvellous. From it she drew mental and physical strength. Here was new beauty, new inspiration. Life stretched before her as interesting and as fathomless as the sea.

CHAPTER II

THE BARRETTS went to Sidmouth expecting to stay two months, and, though they obediently kept themselves poised for flight, it was three years before the parental ukase was issued. The end of their first year found the house that had been pronounced not grand but comfortable an ugly "ruin." Winds blew through the corners and sent tiles crashing into the fireplaces. One chimney had to be pulled down to prevent its tumbling down; and the bricklayers warned the family "not to lean too much out of the windows, for fear the walls should follow the destiny of the chimney."

Mr. Barrett talked of the necessity of moving, especially as the house was not large enough for all his children, and the two sons who had been studying at Glasgow University would soon return. But he was pleased with Sidmouth, "the very land of green lanes and pretty thatched cottages . . . [not] the kind of cottages which are generally thatched, with pigsties and cabbage and dirty children, but thatched cottages with verandas and shrubberies and sounds from the harp or piano coming through the windows . . . The whole valley seems to be thickly wooded down to the very verge of the sea, and these pretty villas to be springing from the ground almost as thickly and quite as naturally as the trees themselves." There were lanes "quite black with foliage, where it is twilight in the middle of the day, and others letting in beautiful glimpses of the spreading heathy hills or of the sunny sea." This was Devonshire at its best. Seeing his children thrive and being himself sensitive to beauty, Mr. Barrett delayed departure.

Elizabeth's health had steadily improved. She was able to accompany her brothers and sisters on donkey-back when they went for long walks. She would sit happily for hours in the bottom of the boat watching the ripples from her brothers' oars. Her cough would disappear for weeks at a time and though she was considered frail she was able in some measure to share the healthful life of her family. Mr. Boyd had come down to the sea, too, and was settled near enough for their Greek readings to continue.

Mr. Barrett's reduced fortune caused Elizabeth no regrets; her life went quietly on, the sea amply compensating her for the loss of Hope End. Her father was kindly disposed; and then he would go away for days at a time. His children honestly thought that they missed him, but they found life full and happy during his absence. Edward went away, too, to Jamaica to investigate the family estates heavily affected by the abolition of colonial slavery.

Missing him, her closest companion, Elizabeth burrowed deeper into Greek, becoming greatly interested in Æschylus until after reading and rereading she tossed off a translation of *Prometheus Bound,* writing furiously and completing the self-imposed task in twelve days. Years later she disdainfully said of this translation that it "should have been thrown into the fire . . . the only means of giving it a little warmth." Had it been so consigned to flames it would not have risen to plague her when fame had come, compelling her finally to write a new version with the hope that this early one would then be forgotten. In 1833, however, she was not alive to its defects; and with pride she saw it issued in a small volume that included also a group of poems much in the vein of her previous publications with a proper dash of love-of-nature and poetic melancholy. The devotion to Byron, which had in her first effort produced a poem on his death, now shone in verses to his infant daughter. The poet was still in the literary workshop. Of her new volume she wrote at its publication, "I dare say I shall wish it out of the light before I have done with it"; yet she was eager to hear her friends' comments, to know if they thought it worthy. She did not consciously present to the world inferior poetry; she did the best of which she was then capable.

The *London Quarterly* in a polite review called the *Prometheus* "a remarkable performance for a young lady but not a good translation in and by itself." Twelve years later she wrote to Mr. Boyd: "Can you guess what I have been doing lately ? Washing out my conscience, effacing the blot on my escutcheon, performing an ex-piation, translating over again from the Greek the *Prometheus* of Æschylus.

"Yes, my dear friend, I could not bear to let that frigid, rigid exercise, called a version and called mine, cold as Caucasus, and flat as the neighbouring plain, stand as my work. A palinodia, a recantation was necessary to me, and I have achieved it."

Not many poets have been either so modest or so painstaking to repair the errors of their youthful verse. Elizabeth Barrett was not one who matured early into intellectual ripeness; neither her teens nor her twenties produced poems that could not easily be spared. Of the *Prometheus* volume she said later: ". . . if my mind had been properly awakened at the time, I might have made still more haste and done it better. Well, the comfort is, that the little book was unadvertised and unknown, and that most of the copies (through my entreaty of my father) are shut up in the wardrobe of his bedroom."

Unbitten by a desire for publicity, Elizabeth published no more for the present, though she continued to write, to read, and to study. Her naturally acquisitive mind, never having been forced into grooves thought proper for young ladies, followed its own paths, wasting little time on frivolities. She tried to understand Prout's *Chemistry,* struggling with the idea of primal matter as indivisible. She turned to the study of Hebrew, finding it for a time more fascinating than Greek.

But the hermit years were drawing to a close. The no longer comfortable house had been sold; Edward was home from Jamaica where the slaves, to Elizabeth's delight, were now virtually free; the two brothers were home from Glasgow where one had successfully won his degree and the other had been prevented by shyness from attempting the examination. Mr. Barrett at last made up his mind to remove his family.

The older boys were ready for some sort of occupation; one would read law in London. Perhaps for this reason, perhaps for no reason at all, Mr. Barrett decided upon London and leased for four months a house at 74 Gloucester Place in which the family was settled in the fall of 1835.

Here was another new world. London was as bad for Elizabeth's health as it was good for her spirits. At last she was to have intellectual companionship and stimulation. At first London, "wrapped up like a mummy, in a yellow mist," did not seem attractive to eyes accustomed to green lanes and stormy seas. Nor was the house, though ample even for the Barrett brood, much of an improvement over the Sidmouth "ruin." While her father investigated unfurnished houses to which he could transfer the Hope End furniture, the months and years went on with Gloucester Place growing more and more uninhabitable.

Elizabeth found amusement in its vicissitudes: "Bro and I were moralizing about shipwrecks, in the dining-room, when down came the chimney through the skylight into the entrance passage. You may imagine the crashing effect of the bricks bounding from the staircase downwards, breaking the stone steps in the process, in addition to the falling in of twenty-four large panes of glass, frames and all. We were terrified out of all propriety, and there has been a dreadful calumny about

Henrietta and me — that we had the hall door open for the purpose of going out into the street with our hair on end, if Bro had not *encouraged* us by shutting the door and locking it. I confess to opening the door, but deny the purpose of it — at least, maintain that I only meant to keep in reserve a way of escape, *in case,* as seemed probable, the whole house was on its way to the ground . . . Sarah the house maid . . . looked up accidentally and saw the nodding chimneys, and ran into the drawing-room to papa, shrieking . . . I never imagined that anything so true to nature as a real live storm could make itself heard in our streets."

Wimpole Street which Mr. Barrett began almost at once to consider (though it took him three years to decide upon it) seemed to Elizabeth a gloomy place where the walls looked like "Newgate's turned inside out." She wilfully chose to disregard the dignity of these tall houses, stressing the monotony of their even roofs and similar façades. Every house displayed an aristocratic front, the ground floor somewhat blank, the first floor with its drawing-room facing the street with long windows, the floors above straight and stolid. From the front windows there was no view except that of the houses across the way, orderly, prim, entirely unexciting. From the back windows one could see only the mews, where occasionally coachmen gossiped as they groomed their horses.

Nevertheless, though her physical horizon narrowed — especially as her health suffered severely under London fogs and family petting — her mental horizon was immeasurably broadened through her new acquaintances. The Victorian literati were not nimble athletes; and Elizabeth Barrett had no need to reform her indolent habits to win their friendship or their respect. Her keen mind, her undoubted critical acumen would have gained their attention in any case; and her sweet kindliness attracted their affection.

Her open sesame to the literary world was John Kenyon, a distant cousin who called early at Gloucester Place to pay his respects to his rhyming relative. The rules of the house permitted his developing an intimacy with Elizabeth without becoming more than an acquaintance of her father. Mr. Barrett chose to ignore the activities of his children when they were not actually in his sight; they might — if they did not talk much about it — make such friends as they chose; but they might not presume to introduce these friends to him without permission; nor might they invite their friends to dinner. In London, Mr. Barrett had developed the habit of vanishing for the greater part of the day; he came and went mysteriously, and in general his children could count upon his absence until late afternoon. His days were spent in "the City" where he occupied himself in speculations; he bought vast quarries; he invested in ships, sending them with cargoes of wool or coal to Odessa, Alexandria, and the far ends of the earth. His evenings were also spent largely away from home in a manner known only to himself; his children did not pry. They were pleased to have their own days and evenings unrestrained.

So Mr. Kenyon became a frequent visitor and a constant correspondent. He had too much wealth to take literature seriously. Under another star he might have been a literary light, but he was content to remain a dilletante, a somewhat casual writer of heroic couplets, and a persistent cultivator of genius. Elegant, courteous, generous, *bon viveur,* and connoisseur of wine, wit, and poetry, he loved to play Mæcenas, gathering at his rich dinner table the most distinguished scholars and writers. An "idealized Pickwick" easily weighing two hundred and fifty pounds, rosy of face and rotund of figure as any brewer, he took naïve pleasure in the patronage of men whose wealth was less than their talent.

Elizabeth, ten years later, tried to explain him to Robert Browning:

And then dear Mr. Kenyon is not even a man of letters in a full sense . . . he is rather a Sybarite of letters. Do you think he ever knew what mental labour is! I fancy not. Not more than he has known what mental inspiration is! And not more than he has known what strife of the heart is . . . with all his tenderness and sensibility. He seems to me to *evade* pain, and where he suffers at all to do so rather negatively than positively . . . rather by a want than by a blow: the secret of all being that he has a certain latitudinarianism (not indifferentism) in his life and affections, and has no capacity for concentration and intensity. Partly by temperament and partly by philosophy he contrives to keep the sunny side of the street — though never inclined to forget the blind man at the corner. Ah, dear Mr. Kenyon: he is magnanimous in toleration, and excellent in sympathy — and he has the love of beauty and the reverence of genius — but the faculty of *worship* he has not: He will not worship aright either your heroes or your gods . . . and while you do it he only "tolerates" the act in you.

Once he said . . . not to me . . . but I heard of it: "What, if genius should be nothing but scrofula ?" and he doubts (I very much fear) whether the world is not governed by a throw of those very same "loaded dice," and no otherwise.   Yet he reveres genius in the acting of it, and recognizes a God in creation — only it is but "so far," and not farther.   At least I think not — and I have a right to think what I please of him, holding him as I do, in such true affection.   One of the kindest and most indulgent of human beings has he been to me, and I am happy to be grateful to him.

Indeed she had cause to be grateful not only at twenty-nine when she entered London unknown, and was introduced by him to celebrities from Wordsworth to Miss Mitford, but much later when he eased her life and Browning's, first by gift of a yearly income and finally by a substantial bequest.   Now her debt to him was purely social.

To the country-bred girl his brilliance of clothes and of conversation were equally astonishing, and his literary acquaintanceship something to marvel at indeed.   Without a trace of vanity he would discourse of his intimate connection with men like Coleridge, Wordsworth, Carlyle, Tennyson.   He dined with everyone of note, and everyone dined with him, his feasts being by far the most lavish.   To one of his magnificent dinners he soon invited Elizabeth, having prepared the ground for her coming by talking of her about town as a most learned female, and a rising young poetess.

Somewhat to her surprise she found herself welcomed by the celebrities that night as one of themselves.   Wordsworth was quite unaware that she trembled with excitement when she acknowledged her introduction to him. Of course he knew that any lady, young or old, must look at him with considerable reverence, but as this young person was a relative of Kenyon's and herself a promising beginner in the art of poetry she was presumably hardened to contacts with the great. He sat beside her and talked long, entertainingly reciting to her Cary's translation of a sonnet of Dante's. Scarce had Elizabeth recovered her equanimity when Walter Savage Landor monopolized her attention. Not to be outdone by Wordsworth he conversed with his undeniable brilliance, taking care to raise his voice so that the room at large might not miss his pointed epigrams and sage remarks. Loud and pompous, he discoursed eloquently about the glory that was Greece. His maganimity led him to present Elizabeth with two Greek epigrams of his own composition. Her brother Edward watched her conquests with much amusement, finally detaching her from Landor that she might mingle with the other guests among whom were a prominent Hebrew scholar appreciative of her knowledge of Hebrew, and the famous Miss Mitford ready to open her arms with effusive friendship for the newcomer.

Mary Russell Mitford was a character in an age that produced characters. At the time that she met Elizabeth Barrett, Miss Mitford was nearly fifty, a dignified, homely little person whose bright eyes sparkled with youthful enthusiasm. Her task it had been for years to support by literary labors herself and the wickedly extravagant father whom she adored. Posterity has forgotten her except as a mildly eccentric person; and is as unmindful of the novels and plays she valued, as of her village sketches whose charm should have granted them longer life. Miss Mitford had her first taste of publicity at the age of ten when she won the lottery prize of twenty thousand pounds, a sum not at all vast enough for her father who, rescued from debtors' prison, dissipated it with surprising rapidity. He was already experienced in the squandering of wealth, having wasted his wife's fortune on cards and bubble stock companies. Nevertheless, to his daughter, in spite of his vulgar tongue, he was a delightful man, guide and mentor of her literary work, and always the joy of her life. She worked long and hard, sacrificing her desire to become "the greatest English poetess," in order to provide money for his bottomless pocket. She was the more drawn to Elizabeth Barrett because here was a young woman well started on the poetical path she would herself have liked to tread.

The two rapidly became the closest of friends, sharing thoughts, ambitions, and pets. It was Miss Mitford who gave Elizabeth the dog, Flush, who became her devoted companion, curling up at the foot of her sofa, keeping quiet while on tiny scraps of paper she wrote in her tiny script the poems that were to make her more famous than Miss Mitford. When Elizabeth needed relaxation Flush would jump down and amuse her; when she was ill he would stay sympathetically by her bedside. When she was well he would scamper outdoors, more than once a prey to the dog-catchers who plied their trade openly in

London, demanding ten guineas' redemption when dog-owners were as fond and as wealthy as tender-hearted Elizabeth.   Whenever Flush disappeared Elizabeth would give up all ordinary occupations, too unhappy to read and write, too miserable to do much but cry.   In such matters she could not reason; she could only feel.   Her joy at recovering Flush the first time, after three days, was tempered by her horror at learning that he had not once been fed; yet, so great was his love of her, that he preferred to press close to her for petting than to gobble his chicken or lap up his macaroons in sugared cream.

Flush's starvation was, however, small reproach to his jailors.   They could hardly have known or sympathized with his eating habits.   He was an overfat wine-colored spaniel completely spoiled by too much attention.   Mr. Barrett complained that Elizabeth had trained Flush in fastidiousness since "no dog in the world could be of his own accord and instinct, so like a woman."   Flush, like the daintiest of non-eating ladies, would apparently scorn food; he would disregard its presence until it was pressed upon him twice or thrice.   Then if the chicken or mutton were roasted, he would eat; if boiled, he would sniff and turn away.   Coffee with muffins he would contentedly lap; coffee without muffins he would scorn.   Macaroons in sugared cream pleased his palate; without the sugar they were anathema.   Generally averse to salt, he demanded salt on his cream cheese and would not eat it unless he personally saw it salted.   His meat he demanded cut fine; and then it must be fed him from a fork.   Such habits did not lead to his happiness when he was stolen or when his mistress was indisposed and her maid lacked time to fuss with him.

Mary Russell Mitford, the giver of Flush, was a kindly soul, effusively friendly, talkative, enthusiastic, romantic, and bustling. Activity was as pleasant to her as it was necessary; she had been forced into busyness to earn a living; and she was one who always seemed busier than she was. She lived "buried in geraniums" and surrounded by pets (the chief being her incorrigible father) about thirty miles from London whither she was always bustling to dine with Kenyon, "the pleasantest man in London," to interview publishers, to visit Elizabeth and fairly wear her out with hours of gay and learned chatter. Miss Mitford knew everyone worth knowing and everything worth reading.

Among Miss Mitford's literary activities was the editing of *Finden's Tableaux,* one of those richly bound annuals which delighted the Victorian heart and decorated Victorian marble tables. Of chief importance were the romantic illustrations: knights on richly caparisoned horses, lordly lovers, lovesick ladies, moonlit gardens, windswept desolate shores, deserts with princely caliphs seated on majestic camels, dying virgins, King Cophetuas and gentle beggar maids. When sufficiently elaborate pictures had been assembled Miss Mitford would trot amiably about among her friends assigning to each a scene about which to write an appropriate poem. If the friend were not at hand she would write:

What I have to request of you is a poem, not shorter than forty or fifty lines, and as much longer as you choose, with a motto from any English poet that you like, on the subject of the enclosed plate — which seems to me to represent a Georgian selling two beautiful girls for a Turkish harem. You may make a story to it if you like, or dwell merely upon their being torn from their country and sent to an unknown land. The terms which my proprietors have enabled me to offer are £5, and a copy of the work, a two-guinea book. But the real advantage is the being included in the most splendid of these works with a very few (there are only eight writers in all) of the choicest poets of the day and sure to be seen upon the table of almost every rich person of taste in England.

Elizabeth, though inclined to doubt the value of such an annual, "gild it as you please," nevertheless was willing to oblige her friend. Her first assignment was a picture of Hindu maidens beside the Ganges River. For it she composed a *Romance of the Ganges* which showed the scholar's inability to write anything however trivial, without investigation of the material and a display of learning; and for the rest a romantic admiration of love-lorn lasses who commit suicide in the presence of successful, though unwitting, rivals. On such fare did annuals thrive.

Miss Mitford was pleased both with the poem and with her new friend. The gushing nature of her friendship did not in any way impair its genuine quality. Elizabeth, nineteen years her junior, was very dear to her. This sweet young woman, delicate in form as in health, fragile in physical beauty, but strong of mind and character, impressed her deeply. Though Elizabeth was thirty at the time of their first meeting she looked like a young girl. Her London acquaintances frequently mistook her for

The Picture for which Elizabeth Barrett Barrett wrote
The Romance of the Ganges

an eighteen-year-old debutante. Her eyes had a soft brightness, her face a gentle expression of absorbed attention that seemed to belong to an unspoiled young girl. An excellent listener, she was popular especially with literary lions, themselves bursting with talk. Had her health permitted and had her father chosen to encourage her social life, Elizabeth would soon have been one of London's most popular dinner guests.

Actually, however, her excursions into the world were few. Her weakness, increased by London fog, her natural modesty and shyness, and her father's peculiarities kept her for the most part at home almost as remote from the world in London as at Hope End. Yet her horizon was widened and the people she did meet gave her a sense of extended literary acquaintanceship. Aside from John Kenyon, the collector of literary lions, and Miss Mitford, who, her white curls bobbing about her rosy face, would retail by the hour tales of her fellow craftsmen, there was the swashbuckling personality of Richard Hengist Horne. Though Elizabeth would not permit Horne to call upon her, pleading ill health, she entered into a close correspondence with him which lasted for twenty years. Only people of considerable leisure could have written or read such interminable letters, long literary discussions that took incalculable hours and reams of letter paper. These were the conversations of people unconcerned with the mechanics of daily life; people whose path was smoothed by the services of underlings.

Of all Elizabeth's new friends Horne was the most exotic. Educated among gentlemen at Sandhurst he early became a midshipman in the Mexican navy during the war with Spain. With his love of war and wandering temporarily satisfied he returned to England, only to find himself under the immediate necessity of earning his living, his patrimony, like that of a hero of romance, dissipated by his guardians. In Victorian England, the first refuge of a stranded gentleman was the profession of letters in which, if he starved, he at least starved genteelly. Horne did not starve. He translated Schlegel, he contributed to magazines, he composed successful tragedies, he wrote two entertaining books for children (both thought worthy of reprint in the twentieth century), he entered the field of biography with a *Life of Napoleon*, he turned out ballads and romances and sundry diversified volumes, he acted as editor of literary magazines, and he contributed to the *Church of England Quarterly*. He wrote an epic greatly admired by Elizabeth; and to show his opinion of England's literary judgments he offered it for sale at a farthing a copy, forbidding its sale to anyone mispronouncing its name, Orion. He became the chief topic of conversation in London drawing-rooms. Many were the theories propounded for his conduct. Mr. Barrett's conjecture seemed to Elizabeth the most ingenious: "Perhaps he is going to shoot the Queen, and is preparing evidence of monomania."

Horne later joined a famous troop of amateur actors. Still later he set out for the Australian gold fields where his talents found a new sphere when he became Chief of Mounted Police and then Gold Commissioner. After seventeen years of pioneering he returned to London and Fleet Street.

Though their correspondence was sedately literary Elizabeth Barrett was by no means unaware of the gossip about him. His eccentricities furnished gaiety for many a tea-table. He was said to make his servant call him at four in the morning though he did not rise until eight. Invited to dinner for Tuesday, he would arrive on Wednesday. At dinner with distinguished people he would attract attention by solemnly pouring libations from the goblets upon his bare head. When gentlemen talked of their dogs and horses he would make mildly insane remarks about holding up a horse by its tail. In the drawing-room he would catapult himself upon a satin sofa and alternately giggle and gabble. He would boast loudly of his income and his "shares" as if he were a plutocrat. He would talk down anyone who ventured to praise Tennyson, considering that poet illustrious mainly by virtue of his being Horne's contemporary. His own genius and fame he graciously admitted; that of other writers he questioned. He would at the mention of popular poems such as "Drink to me only with thine eyes" inquire languidly, "And pray, do tell me who wrote the pretty thing?" Politics he considered altogether beneath his notice, and would elaborately pretend not to know one party from t'other. Somewhat to the scandal of his friends he employed an unknown hack writer to investigate Napoleon and provide him with material which he then used for his *Life of Napoleon*.

All this and more Miss Mitford would retail to the recluse, hardly stopping for breath.   More interesting to the little elderly lady than all Horne's other vagaries was his habit of falling in love freely and rapidly, offering his heart to Miss M (who had fifty thousand pounds) before tea and, being rejected, to Miss N (poorer by but ten thousand pounds) before dinner.   Nothing daunted by another refusal he speedily succumbed to the charms of lesser heiresses, all this in the space of a few days' visit to Miss Mitford, never previously having met any one of the charmers.   Miss Mitford hastened to London to astonish Elizabeth with her correspondent's levity; here was a tale to make a shy invalid gasp.   But though Miss Mitford grew more and more vehement, throwing in details of the ladies' physical or mental deficiencies and the gentleman's indelicate ardor, she could not awaken in her hearer anything stronger than amused tolerance.   Elizabeth had to grant Horne's lack of tact; but she could by no means be made to demolish his character.   And she continued to write him her calm, dispassionate letters.

She had reason to be grateful to Horne for he was directly responsible for her first serious appearance in print. The *Battle of Marathon* was a childish exploit, the *Essay on Mind,* as Coleridge's daughter pronounced it, a mere girl's exercise.   But by the time she had reached thirty Elizabeth Barrett was writing poems which to the Victorian world were of the highest promise.   One of these was sent by a friend to Horne for his criticism. His reply was to send it at once to *Colburn's Magazine,* then edited by Bulwer.   In spite of or because of his eccentricity, Horne was regarded as a critic of note; his endorsement of the poem led to its immediate acceptance. In July 1836 the *Romaunt of Margaret* made its appearance, to be followed in October by *The Poet's Vow*. Now at last Elizabeth Barrett was fairly launched as a poet.

CHAPTER III

AT A TIME of literary activity all writers profit by the public interest. Public expectancy of greatness grants justice to many a poet who as a lone voice crying in the wilderness would never have been heard. In a poetically arid period Elizabeth Barrett's flute might have played to the empty air. Moxon, the authoritative publisher, swore that the more poetry he published the more money he lost, Tennyson alone being for him a profitable gamble. But so have publishers always sworn; and so swearing have prospered.

Elizabeth Barrett had no need to live by her pen; yet even the most enthusiastic writer prefers to be published rather than to issue his poems or prose at his own expense. It was with a real thrill that Elizabeth prepared her new volume of poetry — *The Seraphim and Other Poems* — which was given to the world in 1838, admitting her to fellowship with Bulwer, Horne, Hunt, Landor, Wordsworth, Tennyson (who was three years her junior), Mrs. Hemans, and Browning.

Joy was, however, tempered by many an untoward circumstance. The death of a well-loved uncle was not the less a deep grief because of her pecuniary gain. By his fondness for her she became the possessor of an income of some four hundred pounds a year, the only one of the Barretts to be thus independent of the father. The significance of this independence did not mean much to her at the time, but was in a few years to be the means of giving her everything that made her life memorable. Now she could only grieve, while her health became rapidly worse under the inhospitable London climate.

Having moved to London, Mr. Barrett did not choose to permit his family to stir.   Excursions to the seashore for the summer or to milder skies for the winter were suggested, discussed, discussed and suggested.   Nothing ever happened.   His children though mature did not dare to push the matter to a definite yes or no.   They waited hopefully, despairingly.   The boys from time to time after causing a volcanic upheaval in the household would wrest trips to the Rhine, to Jamaica, to Switzerland. Even Henrietta escaped for months to friends and Torquay.   Elizabeth remained without change until finally a serious illness, which she believed to be the bursting of a bloodvessel on the lungs, turned her into a complete invalid.   Now for a long time she was bedridden, fainting even over the exertion of being lifted to the sofa while her bed was changed.   Doctors looked grave, oversaw leeches and blisters, prescribed various nauseous and worthless doses along with the two medicinal certainties, digitalis and opium.   Finally, in 1838, Mr. Barrett yielded to the physician's insistence and permitted Elizabeth's removal from London.   Mr. Barrett, now as later, was not quite sure that Elizabeth's illnesses were unavoidable. His native shrewdness more than suspected that a diet of good beefsteak and porter would remedy the defects of a constitution nourished on dry toast and feminine delicacies. Doctors, he declared, got their livelihood reconciling foolish women to their follies. However he made no strenuous objections to her pampering, and himself brought from the booksellers the most recent mental delicacies.

At length he gave his permission for her removal to Torquay where she, attended by one of her sisters, would stay with an aunt. He himself would visit her from time to time; and perhaps she would benefit by the change. Torquay certainly ought to help her, if she needed help. The mild air ought to entice her outdoors where she would do much better than lolling on a sofa indoors. Once she saw that bay, blue as Naples, flanked by green hills from which the white buildings gleamed she would want to grow strong, to be abroad enjoying such beauty. Her best loved brother, Edward, was courier for the journey, with orders to return to London immediately upon seeing his sisters comfortably settled. When time for parting came Elizabeth grew tearful; Edward had no pressing duties in London; he did not, like the younger boy, read law; why could he not remain at Torquay with her and make her recovery the more certain ? Their aunt took it upon herself to interfere, writing Mr. Barrett in such a way that he felt forced to yield, albeit ungraciously. He considered the request unworthy of Elizabeth; but since she demanded such indulgence, why let her take it. His message to her left her in no doubt as to his anger.

Edward found Torquay with his fond sister and without his imperious father wholly delightful. He was a likable young man of sociable habits. Elizabeth, to be sure, was not strong enough for parties and balls, but she was too reasonable to tie him to her bedside. She enjoyed his tales of the gay young people with whom he danced and dined, sailed and swam. Henrietta sometimes joined him in these merry times, when Arabel took her turn staying with the invalid whom for weeks at a time the doctors would keep in bed. Mr. Barrett's disapproval of Edward's remaining did not prevent his frequently coming to Torquay to make sure that Elizabeth was paying due regard to her poetry, and Edward getting into as little mischief as possible.

There was no more talk of Edward's leaving; and, though Elizabeth really believed that her father's presence was an aid to both her health and her happiness, she did not grieve over the prolonging of convalescence. For the most part she and Edward were peacefully content, though now and again a cloud would come between them, since rarely can brother and sister live in perfect accord. It was on a day when they had had some slight disagreement and had parted with somewhat "pettish" words that Edward and some other young men went sailing by themselves, all being perfectly capable of handling a boat.

Elizabeth watched them sail out into the harbor, inclined to moan her fate. It was all very well to be the centre of attention, to be petted and praised, to have all possible time for one's beloved books, and all possible leisure for testing one's poetical powers. It was delightful to see one's words in a fine volume, and read serious discussion of one's poems in leading Reviews; but still it would be pleasant not always to be forgotten in hours of pleasure and relaxation. Perhaps after all Edward's was the better lot.

Her anxiety in the late afternoon was still somewhat mixed with other emotions — a little crossness remaining from the morning, a large regret for having been childish, a longing to have Edward return that their relationship might be restored to its normal tranquillity. As night came and went with no news of the boat or its sailors the anxiety grew unbearable. It seemed absurd, weak, foolishly feminine to believe in disaster. The three young men were perfectly able seamen; they were strong and healthy. Could they not be gone overnight without their womenfolk going into a panic ? Round and round went her mind, outlining possibilities, insisting to itself that any one was more plausible than drowning. The tears that she could not restrain she despised as childishly unreasonable. Both her sisters were with her then; they pulled aside the curtains at the window, trying to reassure themselves and her by the mirror-smoothness of the sea.

In the morning tears seemed foolish; the sun shone, the blue sea glistened, there were boats coming in to the harbor, many of them also having been gone all night. Such a calm and dreamily beautiful sea could hurt no one, they told themselves. They tried to allay their aunt's worry; they tried to eat and talk and work as usual. Young men did foolish things; with a trusty boat they could go far; and soon they would come sailing in with a laughing tale of adventure; young men did not like to be tied to their womenfolk's apronstrings; they must have their bursts of freedom, even as Flush who would tug at the leash until he broke away and had a lawless run. This was an adventure, nothing more. So they told themselves. But when two days had gone by, when Mr. Barrett had come, when all the streets and wharves of Torquay had been placarded with offers of reward for anything, even so much as a handkerchief, to give certainty of the young sailors' fate, then there could be no more pretence of doubt. Not only would Edward never come back, but there would be nothing remaining for a memento, not a lock of hair, not a lowly mound, or the humblest gravestone. When, after three days, his body was found the last feeble hope ended.

Now there was no strength left for tears. Elizabeth's collapse was complete; she could not even talk. Completely bowed down with grief over the loss of her brother she was still further oppressed by her father who stood as external conscience, by his very silence saying, "This was thy deed!" Had he not written that Edward might remain with her at Torquay but that she was entirely wrong to exact that permission of him? And had she not persisted, thinking more of her own immediate comfort than of her duty to her father? She had kept Edward at Torquay; she and she alone was responsible for depriving her father of his eldest son. She had disregarded her father's wishes; and in a most awful way had been taught that as always he knew best. The very fact that he forbore to reproach her verbally made her writhe the more — as he very well knew. Had he burst forth into reproaches her spirits would have risen under the injustice of his complaints; for although she had detained Edward at Torquay she had not sent him to his death. Her father's generous forbearance — he knew it was generous and she acknowledged freely that it was — made it quite evident that he believed her wholly responsible. His unusual patience with her in her now dangerous illness made the more dramatic his kindness and her guilt. And yet he did not mean to be unkind. He could not say to her things he did not believe; he could not comfort her by telling her that it was not her fault; that even had she never gone to Torquay Edward might have been drowned; he did not believe this himself. Elizabeth had persuaded Edward to his death; that was the only interpretation he could make of events. He was sorry to see her ill; he would grieve if she died; but the misfortune which was more his than hers had been of her bringing. It was a hard lesson for her, he felt, but if she lived she must profit by it.

Mr. Barrett was a sternly religious man. He had to make the most of disasters. Parental authority was Biblical; it was the basis of religion. First came the authority of a heavenly Father; second only to that the authority of an earthly father. In this case tribulation was directly due to Elizabeth's interference with the authority of her earthly father; and upon her had fallen the swift punishment from Heaven.

It is small wonder that in such an atmosphere Elizabeth

failed to rally either in mind or body for many months; or that for the rest of her life she shuddered at the faintest mention of her brother Edward.   There was an inevitable morbidity in her memory, caused partly by her brooding over her unfriendly parting with Edward, not knowing that there would never again be a meeting, but largely by her father's attitude.   Years later she forced herself to tell the story (with a brevity not usual in her letters) to Robert Browning, asking him never in any way to refer to the matter to her or to anyone.   When Miss Mitford in her *Recollections of a Literary Life* referred to the incident in her slight sketch of Elizabeth's life, Elizabeth wrote her a strong protest exhibiting genuine agony. From the time of her recovery Edward's name was banned.

Her only relief from this morbidity she found later in *De Profundis,* a poem strong and true in rhythm and feeling.   In her utter despair she would have welcomed death; and had her youthful agnosticism not been displaced by a belief in a loving God, she could not willingly have faced a return to life.   But after months of practically suspended animation she did slowly recover, believing, as her family and her physicians now believed, that from this time forward invalidism was her portion.   Perhaps she felt that in permanently renouncing health she was in some way making expiation.

Whatever the motive she accepted invalidism; and both from a desire to leave the place where the waves monotonously beat into her head "Edward is gone, Edward is gone, is gone, is gone," and from a desire to make her martyrdom complete, she began to fret for London where presumably she could never be well. "Ah !" she wrote Horne, "when I was ten years old, I beat you all — you and Napoleon and all — in ambition; but now I only want to get home." Eventually in the fall of 1841 she returned to London, travelling in an invalid's carriage with specially contrived bedsprings against the jolting of twenty-five miles a day.

And now came the years of self-immolation when during the winter Elizabeth not only never left her room but never swallowed one breath of fresh air. With brown paper thoroughly sealing every crack about the window-panes, and with the door most carefully shut — visitors would slide in through the veriest crack swiftly mended by the gentle shutting of the door — Elizabeth's world shrank. The room was not light to begin with, and it was kept dimmer with curtains. It did not face the street or have any sort of desirable outlook. Before the window, when warm weather permitted its opening, hung a transparent blind, with a castle on it, and "a castle gateway, and two walks, and several peasants, and groves of trees which rise in excellent harmony with the fall of my green damask curtains . . . Papa insults me with the analogy of a back window in a confectioner's shop, but is obviously moved when the sunshine lights up the castle, notwithstanding. And Mr. Kenyon and everybody in the house grow ecstatic rather than other-wise, as they stand in contemplation before it, and tell me (what is obvious without their evidence) that the effect is beautiful, and that the whole room catches a light

The Picture for which Elizabeth Barrett Barrett
wrote *The Dream*

from it.   Well, and then Mr. Kenyon has given me a new table, with a rail round it to consecrate it from Flush's paws, and large enough to hold all my varieties of vanities."

John Kenyon constantly did his best to brighten Elizabeth's room, sending ivy to grow in boxes outside the window to create a sense of the green world, and primroses to bloom within.   But flowers could not thrive in air thought proper for a human being.   In this close atmosphere Elizabeth lay weeks at a time, on her better days being lifted to the sofa where she and Flush curled up on silken cushions.   When she was strong enough to be dressed, her maid would array her in rich velvet and laces; and the picture that met the eyes of her few visitors was indeed attractive — dainty, fragile Elizabeth with her pretty face no longer vivid with fresh coloring, but romantically pale, looking more gently mature, less innocently childish, with wine-colored silky Flush at her feet.   Victorians were used to close rooms; and John Kenyon and Miss Mitford could sit long hours in Elizabeth's stifling atmosphere conversing brilliantly.   Elizabeth could lie there day after day, week after week, without any appreciable decline of her intellectual powers.   She found it necessary to take a nightly dose of opium to induce sleep, however.   By day she read Greek, wrote erudite or chatty letters, and composed poetry.

Her first refuge from her thoughts while she was still at Torquay had been work, reading, thinking, writing.   She felt that she would surely go mad if she did not keep her mind thoroughly occupied.   Not being an exact scholar, she could not find balm in meticulous research. Hers was rather the creative talent which makes use of older literature as a basis for independent thought.

As soon as her strength had rallied from the shock of Edward's death she began both to read and to write, finding the classics a surer refuge than the novels that at other times had furnished relaxation. So perturbed was her physician to find his patient bent over pages of Greek, so puzzled was he at such a fancy on the part of a lady, that to save him anxiety she had her favorite set of Plato bound modishly to resemble fashionable novels. He looked at the fine binding and was relieved to find his patient presumably seeking lighter fare. This was the first step toward recovery — the regaining of a sense of humor, a slight showing of the gaiety natural to her.

Here Horne furnished her with a safe outlet. He was unknown to her personally, a friend, indeed, but one only so intellectually. To him she could write because to him she need never mention personal matters, except her health, and this because of its occasional interruption of their correspondence or work together, and also because health is naturally a matter of absorbing interest to any invalid. Of far greater interest were Horne's new books, especially his latest "grand" tragedy. Mr. Barrett brought her these new books, hoping to interest her, for he had no wish to lose this child, too. And they did interest her to the point of a gentle quarrel with Horne on the function of tragedy and its relation to the stage, she holding that the union of tragedy and the stage was only less incongruous and absurd than the union of church and state.

Struggling against sadness she inclined to supplant it by levity, becoming, as Mr. Kenyon declared, "fairly insolent" on paper. Certainly her letters even from Torquay sparkled with good spirits. She teased Mr. Horne freely, especially on his curious scheme of rejuvenescence, as she persisted in calling his attack of whooping cough. There was, perhaps, a fear on Elizabeth's part of becoming too completely blue-stocking; hence in her letters she constantly veered off from the intellectual discussions which were the main reason for her correspondence with Horne. She was collaborating with him in various critical essays on contemporary authors; sometimes she wrote practically the whole essay, sometimes merely emended his. He took her criticisms and suggestions seriously, realizing their justice and their insight. Her work was anonymous, Horne assuming full responsibility and accepting the avalanche of praise and blame heaped upon the publication. Elizabeth had much private mirth from her friends' discussion of the essays, and much pleasure when they praised some bit of her own.

Miss Mitford at this time felt a change in Elizabeth; her conversation which had previously smelt too much of the lamp became more normally human. It still was weighted with learning; it still betrayed a wider reading than that of her audience; but it sparkled with wit, and its whole tone was lighter. Elizabeth's first real contact with grief, then, led to a softening of character. She might have been betrayed into bitterness, or into spineless self-sacrifice, or into mere complaining femininity. Instead she developed in serenity and in self-sufficiency.

The result was a deepening of her poetic powers and an increase in production. A volume all but ready for publication (Moxon's reluctance being overcome) in 1843 was held up by her fancy to finish "a fragment of a sort of mask on *The First Day's Exile from Eden*" for which she desired first place in the book. When in 1844 this was completed as the *Drama of Exile* it was found that no single volume of suitable slimness could hold all the new poems. Moxon therefore decreed a two-volume edition, rudely suggesting rearrangements to make the volumes of equal length. Elizabeth had her own idea of these things, having her heart set, for instance, on having *The Dead Pan* for concluding poem. Therefore there was nothing to do but to add something to volume one. She was not in the habit of writing hurriedly or of publishing without careful revisions. It was with amusement that she seized upon an unfinished poem and in one day composed the hundred and forty long lines necessary for its completion. She was still more amused when the critics singled out this frantic production, *Lady Geraldine's Courtship,* for special praise.

For the critics who had treated the 1838 volume with kind but patronizing tolerance now "sounded a clarion" for England's foremost poetess. At the same time an American edition won almost instant popularity and the extravagant praise of Edgar Allan Poe, who hastened to dedicate a volume of collected tales and poems to this new literary light. In his dedication he called her the "noblest of her sex." What, she queried, ought she to say in thanking him ? "Sir, you are the most discerning of yours." In spite of her modesty and her tendency to jest she knew that this at last was Fame. She, who lived apart from the world, who observed but did not share its activities, who ventured forth only in the mildest weather to see grass and trees and people on the street, who for weeks at a time lay quietly in bed visited only now and then by brothers and sisters, her father, and a mere handful of friends, she, country bred, weak, untravelled, unknown, and a woman, was now deemed fit to stand beside the poets she most loved and respected.

CHAPTER IV

BUT FAME, however pleasant, cannot much alter a life spent in seclusion. To Elizabeth Barrett in her dim chamber where no clock ticked, the passing of time marked only by the coming and going of the family, and the arrival of meals, fame at first meant little more than an increase of parental praise and a still greater increase in her mail as unknown admirers poured forth their appreciation and piled up requests for autographs and verses for young ladies' albums. From her walls smiled down upon her the framed pictures of Harriet Martineau, Wordsworth, Tennyson, Carlyle, and Browning. She knew Harriet Martineau; she had met and conversed with Wordsworth, she had exchanged a letter or so with Tennyson; but Browning was unknown to her save as his verses spoke for him. To be sure her physically ponderous and mentally nimble cousin, John Kenyon, often amused her by anecdotes of Browning whom he knew fairly well, having indeed been a schoolmate of Browning's father. And she had been bold enough to show her love of his poems; for in *Lady Geraldine's Courtship,* written while he was publishing his *Bells and Pomegranates,* she had her poet-lover read aloud:

. . . Wordsworth's solemn-thoughted idyl,
Howitt's ballad-verse, or Tennyson's enchanted reverie, —

Or from Browning some "Pomegranate," which, if cut deep
   down the middle,
Shows a heart within blood-tinctured, of a veined humanity.

And so when the year 1845 opened for her with a
letter from Robert Browning her heart leapt as she read
its very first words: "I love your verses with all my heart,
dear Miss Barrett." And though he wrote in prose she
was not dull to the poetry of his letter reiterating as it
did, "I do, as I say, love these books with all my heart —
and I love you, too." And once John Kenyon had offered
to introduce Browning to Elizabeth Barrett but she had
then been too unwell to receive a stranger; "and now it
is years ago, and I feel as at some untoward passage in
my travels, as if I had been close, so close, to some world's-
wonder in chapel or crypt, only a screen to push and I
might have entered, but there was some slight, so it now
seems, slight and just sufficient bar to admission, and the
half opened door shut, and I went home my thousands of
miles, and the sight was never to be ?" This was stronger
language, and sweeter, than that of even her American
admirers whose praise was amply extravagant. The personal note did not frighten her. The frail invalid who
trembled in nervous terror at the very thought of meeting
a stranger, was never afraid of written superlatives. She
had for years, refusing to see Richard Horne, conversed
gaily and familiarly with him on paper. So now to a
man like Browning, a man whom she had not seen, she
could answer at once with the utmost friendliness. Her
natural mode of expression was with pen and paper;
when she talked she was sometimes stilted; when she

wrote she was at once intimate and unreserved. Her quiet life had preserved her youthfulness; she saw no reason for not replying instantly to this pleasant letter with the flippant remark that had Browning entered his "crypt" he "might have caught cold, or been tired to death, and *wished* himself 'a thousand miles off.' " And though in winter she was a veritable dormouse, still spring would come and then perhaps . . . Meanwhile she professed herself his most devout admirer.

At this time Elizabeth Barrett was nearing forty. Except for her best-loved brother's death emotion had touched her lightly. When that brother had fallen in love she had tried to understand his feelings; so deep was the sympathy between the two that herein she approached, she thought, the nearest she could to actual love. For she was no ascetic. Romantic she had always been from the time when she had dreamed of being Lord Byron's page. She actually hated Lady Byron who, possessing the great poet's love, did neither value nor keep it. Byron was one thing, however; the few young men who, attracted by the beauty and charm of the Barrett sisters or their father's wealth, hovered round her and her sisters were another kettle of fish. Henrietta, the gay sister who dearly loved a waltz or a polka, who even dared to give a dance in the Wimpole Street house when her father was providentially out of town, attracted young men as honey does flies. Arabel, the more serious-minded, had her quiver of young curates. And frail Elizabeth herself did not lack lovers. She was, so said her sisters, entirely too romantic; nothing short of a Lord Byron would ever suit her.   She wanted this and that; unswerving devotion, unquestioning adoration, and a perfection unheard of in masculinity.   Henrietta was less hard to satisfy, years ago having readily attached herself to a fond lover though dutifully refusing to bind herself without the parental consent.   The unoffending young man at her bidding threw himself at the rock of Mr. Barrett's monomania — for so John Kenyon called his absolute prohibition of marriage.   Even a prince or princess of the blood, come courting with most honorable proposals and the wealth of Indies, would not have been welcomed by Mr. Barrett. What Mr. Barrett's experiences had been to thus make him completely the enemy of marriage one cannot tell; certainly his refusals in all cases were adamant.   Edward had been powerless to disobey, having neither fortune nor profession to rely upon for livelihood; and gentle Elizabeth's offer to transfer to him her modest but competent fortune was angrily vetoed by the autocrat of the family.

Henrietta's lover ventured to ask her father for her hand.   Whether or not he left the room mentally and physically unimpaired is unknown.   Probably Henrietta never dared even inquire.   For Mr. Barrett strode into the bosom of his family, having previously lashed himself up into a state of violent anger most satisfying to its possessor and most devastating to those who had meekly to suffer its effects.   Henrietta, being made of soft substance, wilted at once, sobbed and begged pardon.   Elizabeth, always nervously tense, listened to the scathing denunciations, the almost insane threats, with true terror.

She knew full well that had she been in Henrietta's place she would have been unable to enact Henrietta's part; she would have had to defend herself and her loved one; she could not have thus passively relented. With her, emotions were too deeply rooted to be torn up at bidding. And so, while Henrietta sought release in tears, Elizabeth, imaginatively putting herself in the culprit's place, sank quietly to the floor in a faint.

Henrietta recovered, taking refuge in clandestine gaieties, and solacing herself with the attentions of new admirers, three of whom were soon forming a little court about her, much to the amusement of her sisters and brothers and quite without the knowledge of Mr. Barrett who believed that he had once and for all settled this marriage business. Elizabeth, now feeling that Henrietta was probably incapable of true, deep, and lasting love, felt no more concern, and laughingly watched the comedy. Henrietta, she knew, would not fall in love; but she would continue to be touched by men's love of her. She would always find it difficult to refuse an ardent lover and would forever have her half-yes interpreted into a full yes, until the question came up of consulting her father. Admiration she could not resist; and of her three lovers she was not sure which she preferred until one of them withdrew from the uncertain contest consoling himself by dubbing his rivals "Perseverance and Despair." Joining Elizabeth and Arabel as audience in the drama he now saw Despair seemingly marked for winner. For though Despair's proposal was rejected, the rejection was so mild and sweet that it soon was turned to a half-consent. Despair, so the brothers said, was "a gentleman at least"; which Perseverance was not. And hence he suffered as all gentlemen must when they feel that they cannot retaliate against impertinent Perseverance. Poor Despair speedily found himself "elbowed . . . into the open streets," too genteel to elbow his way back again to the parlor where Perseverance sat boldly declaring that it was he whom Henrietta loved — though she did not yet know it — and that "if she married another he would wait till she became a widow, trusting to Providence," and looking as if he knew just whose sword Providence would use. Despair wilted and ran, preferring a whole skin to a half-willing lady.

Perseverance sat for hours on end, disregarding the coming and going of brothers and sisters, wholly immune to black looks and rude words. He would lurk unseen until Mr. Barrett would start off each day on his journey to the city and would then pay his determined visits, once a week marking time by a definite proposal of marriage. And regularly when his proposals were rejected he would burst into hysterical weeping quite unsuitable in an officer; weeping caused by such genuine emotion that he could not restrain it even in public. Whether he were alone with Henrietta or in the presence of members of her family, even if visitors came at that unfortunate moment, his tears flowed on. Henrietta forgot Despair as he had forgotten her — for he bought a new horse and began music lessons to assuage his grief — and being of unresisting metal, suffered him to adore her so long as Mr. Barrett was uninformed.

And this was all Elizabeth saw of love. When she questioned her brothers she found that they saw nothing extraordinary in this mistaking attachment for love. Their married friends, even those who were happily married, would sometimes tell them that they had ruined their prospects by marriage or that in spite of happiness with their wives they would have done better to marry elsewhere. Self-love, pity, admiration, blind impulse, these things went current in the world for the gold coin of romance.

And yet somewhere romance might exist. Perhaps some time even for her the fairy prince might come riding — but no; she was too weak, too insignificant; and then she would demand too much. She could not content herself with a substitute like Henrietta.

Meantime she was free to dream of love as romantically as she pleased. Devouring romances — she jestingly spoke of her epitaph as the "world's greatest novel reader" — she enjoyed vicariously many a passionate love cycle. Occasionally she let her fancy burst into rhyme. So in *The Romaunt of the Page* we have lovely lady following incognita her knightly husband and gently but resolutely suffering death at the hands of the Paynims, when she learns from his own lips that he would consider such unfeminine conduct unpardonable in wife of his. In the popular *Lady Geraldine's Courtship* the poet, poor in all but his art, wins the love of the rich and courted beautiful maiden. In the *Rhyme of the Duchess May* the fair lady having wed the man of her choice climbs up on his horse and rides to death with him when her rejected suitor storms and takes the castle. Gentle Bertha in *Bertha in the Lane* dies that her sister, younger by seven years, may be happy with the lover who once thought he loved her. And Catarina, dying, sings mournfully to the absent Camoens whose poem had called hers the sweetest eyes ever seen. These unreal heroics were the delight of the Victorian reading public; they were even the delight of fellow poets like Robert Browning who signalled them out for special praise when he wrote their author.

They more nearly described Elizabeth's dreams of what love might be than her actual beliefs. For she looked on Henrietta and wrote *The Lady's Yes:*

"Yes," I answered you last night;
   "No," this morning, sir, I say:
Colors seen by candle-light
   Will not look the same by day.

When the viols played their best,
   Lamps above and laughs below,
Love me sounded like a jest,
   Fit for *yes* or fit for *no*.

Yet the sin is on us both;
   Time to dance is not to woo;
Wooing light makes fickle troth,
   Scorn of *me* recoils on *you*.

Learn to win a lady's faith
   Nobly, as the thing is high,
Bravely, as for life and death,
   With a loyal gravity . . .

This for Henrietta. Differently she judged herself, dreaming of one standing by the river where once a lover stood, too:

I stand by the river, I think of the vow;
Oh, calm as the place is, vow-breaker, be thou!

. . . . . .

Go, be sure of my love, by that treason forgiven;
Of my prayers, by the blessings they win thee from Heaven;
Of my grief — (guess the length of the sword by the sheath's)
By the silence of life, more pathetic than death's!
        Go, — be clear of that day!

Here is no hint of deep feeling for love, only the thought that such an emotion if carried to its deepest would be something other than the emotions she saw in friends and family, wooed or wedded. Only in the poem *Loved Once* does she sound a stronger note as she broods on the bitterness of the phrase "I loved once":

But love strikes one hour — LOVE! Those *never* loved
Who dream that they loved ONCE.

Only very little was the ground prepared for the foot-steps of an impetuous lover, so far had she to go from these maidenly dreamings to the passionate reality of the *Sonnets from the Portuguese*. She was never one to complain; she might feel that life had passed her by without abating one jot of the "cheerfulness taught by reason" upon which she preferred to lean. She never permitted herself a word of reproach when her brothers forgot to visit her in her seclusion; she grieved but let no one know of her grieving. So, too, when Mr. Barrett overlooked her instead of paying his regular nightly visit, to say prayers by her bedside, she never asked for reason. She saw uncomplainingly the drama of life pass her by:

> I think we are too ready with complaint
> In this fair world of God's . . .

she sang, and again:

> We overstate the ills of life, and take
> Imagination (given us to bring down
> The choirs of singing angels overshone
> By God's clear glory) down our earth to rake
> The dismal snows instead, flake following flake,
> To cover all the corn; we walk upon
> The shadow of hills across a level thrown,
> And pant like climbers: . . .

The "wisdom of cheerfulness" was the creed that made her happy. She lay in her unaired room, dressed in velvets and laces, waited upon by an adoring maid, attended by silky wine-colored Flush who curled himself gracefully at her feet ready to spring up and amuse her when her eyes were weary with reading and writing. To her came at times relatives and friends; and constantly a stream of incense-burning letters from friends and strangers. She was treated as a piece of rare and fragile statuary and somehow managed to keep her soul from shrinking under this system of patronizing adoration.

But of all her letters none came with such a breathless rush as these of her fellow poet, Robert Browning.

Here was one whom she had long admired, feeling as if on herself every lash of the critics' whips. Superstitiously she cherished the fact that though England praised her and rejected Browning, America welcomed them with equal ardor. As she read his poems she felt a closer bond than that which drew her to any other of her contemporaries. With her infinite leisure she was happy to enter into correspondence with him, each pouring forth on paper interminably long conversations, first praises of the other's poetry, then disquisitions on anything and everything, but always lengthy excursions into the meaning of this or that phrase in the last letter. He would rather write to her, he soon declared, than see anyone else. Only people with no fixed occupations could thus keep up a rapid backfire of compliments in cryptic phrases interlarded with poetic lore and critical acumen, letter following letter with bewildering speed until the intimacy became deeper and deeper, though definitions of "Spring" when they should meet in the flesh still differed. Browning saw spring before the first of February, but Elizabeth, happy in this new and dearest of friends, rejoicing in the freedom from restraint, the freedom almost of anonymity, put spring forward to May.

Actually, she was somewhat vexed with him for demanding to see her. The best of her, she had always felt, was on paper; personally she was nothing to see, nothing to enjoy. Her tongue tripped in vocal conversation; it was only when curled up on her sofa with the silent companionship of Flush that she could express what she truly felt. Then she could be gay and familiar and perhaps interesting; and all without effort. Besides, people who came and stared — as in spite of her fears and prohibitions they sometimes did — as if she were one of the wonders of the world or a specimen of some extinct species — bored her. She could gloat over *Pippa Passes* and covet its authorship in private; she could from the sure seclusion of her room write Browning how deeply she felt about it; but could she look at him and say the half of that ? Why, after all, should what promised to be an enjoyable friendship, an exchange of ideas literary and human, be interfered with by physical nearness ?

She had, indeed, as a result of her secluded life, a somewhat exaggerated idea of the values of social intercourse; she recoiled from testing her ideas on the score of her frailty. She had so long thought of herself as a sort of Marianna of the Moated Grange that she could not accept visitors simply. The announcement of a visit from the most polite of old ladies would upset her day and leave her breathless and tired even when she listened rather than talked. Mr. Kenyon amused her, to be sure; but such amusement needed to be in distant doses. She saw herself fragile, incapable of coping with the world of boisterous men and women. And she settled rather contentedly into the niche of the shrine her family had made for her.

And now this new friend wished to view her. Secretly she felt that this desire to push into her "crypt" showed a lack of fineness in his nature. She had thought him different from other people; and here he was after all of common clay. His exuberance of admiration and devotion she laughingly assigned to poetic exaggeration, and to his earnest pleas for a recognition of the presence of spring — when the promised interview was due — she answered steadily that for her spring was not yet while east winds blew.

Nevertheless, she could not bring herself to risk the termination of this friendship already dearer to her far than that of any other, by direct denial of his request. Spring would come, she promised. And it was not without a blush and a thrill of delight that she read his bold, "But if my truest heart's wishes avail, as they have hitherto done, you shall laugh at east winds yet, as I do," signing himself emphatically "Yours *ever.*" This was strong language pleasant to read quietly in uneventful days. When he saw her he would, of course, speak differently. She feared that he had built up a romantic notion of her that would suffer when he saw her, pale, nervous little thing, lying motionless on her couch. Once she knew she had been pretty with what her friends called unusually lovely coloring; that had all gone in her grief over Edward. Now she was one to awake pity, not admiration; and pity was not the basis for true friendship. From her wall Browning's portrait looked kindly upon her; would that face, full of vigor and vitality, look as kindly upon her in the actual flesh ? He who lived a normal life among vigorous men and women might come to despise her when he saw her the weakling she was. Well, but he must have his way, silly boy — why could he not be sensible ?

And so finally the day was appointed. Wilson, the

adoring maid, selected the newest and finest velvet gown, the daintiest of lace frills; the soft brown curls were brushed till they glistened; Flush was properly groomed and instructed; the stage was set and Wilson, looking with pleasure upon her pretty mistress, turned to the door only to be called back for one more task.

"I think," said Elizabeth rapidly to cover her embarrassment, "I think I'd rather you removed that picture of Mr. Browning.   Put it in my desk drawer.   Yes, it would never do to let the young gentleman know we hung him with Wordsworth and Tennyson. . ."

And promptly at three o'clock like an impetuous boy, Robert Browning knocked at the door to be ushered into the dim room to feast his eyes on the poet he already loved. New incense he brought from any she had ever learned; incense that left behind a heady and persisting aroma.

For all his thirty-three years Browning was essentially boyish.   Under quite different circumstance from Elizabeth's illnesses and seclusion he had somehow managed to preserve the same youthful outlook, combined in his case with buoyancy and headlong enthusiasm. He had lived always in the happiest of circumstances with unusually understanding and devoted parents, all his poetic strivings and ideas encouraged and understood. He had not, like Elizabeth, been put upon a pedestal with his earliest babyish lispings engraved upon it; but he had been given every opportunity to find himself and develop the talents that were in him. He had gone to school with other boys; he had studied as much as he liked at

London University. He had travelled to Russia and to Italy. So far his only disappointment in life had been his failure to win a coveted diplomatic post; but that was nothing to disturb him deeply. For the rest, as he naïvely boasted, life always gave him those things upon which he set his heart. He wrote, as Elizabeth did, from inner conviction, and whether critics were kind or cruel mattered not much. He wrote to satisfy himself, and in the end the world would see, would judge between him and these blind critics. Sure he was of himself though not conceited. Elizabeth, he felt, had a right to conceit; there was no sense in her modesty, she who wrote like the very angels.

This was the bond between them, this dedication of life to poetry. In this they were supremely alike; in all else their lives parted sharply. For he was definitely of the world, a lively young man who rode and walked, travelled and danced, doing all with the vigor of youth and health, thoroughly alive to mundane joys. He was a voluble talker, his words coming a bit too fast and loud for fastidious Victorians. In the drawing-room he was somewhat obvious both because of his unsubdued animation and because of his good looks. Ladies languished and longed for a glance from his soft eyes; they admired his dark hair, his shapely hands (with or without the lemon gloves he affected), his pleasant if not wholly polished manners, his gay compliments, and his boyish enjoyment of the dances they willingly granted.

He went about having a thoroughly good time, heart whole and fancy free. Utterly devoted to his mother

ROBERT BROWNING
At 23

ELIZABETH BARRETT AS A GIRL
Drawn by her sister Arabella

he saw in all women something to love and to reverence. As a boy, he had fervently admired a young lady older than he by nearly a decade, Eliza Haworth, whose sister composed the hymn *Nearer My God to Thee*. Other women, too, he had admired; none had he loved. He had come to think himself excluded from affairs of the heart except as he imaginatively loved with the characters in his poetical romances and dramas.

Love to Browning, however, was strongly passionate, not sentimentally languishing as it was in Elizabeth Barrett's poems. His lovers kiss their souls out "in a burning mist." They cling mouth to hot mouth; they gaze each upon the other

> . . . till I change, grow you — I could
> Change into you, beloved !

They are athirst for each other, body and soul; their souls rush together; they scarce can breathe so close they hold. And when death overtakes them they can say that they

Having lived indeed, and so — (yet one more kiss) can die !

Thus did Browning envisage love before he personally felt its power. And to such an emotionally receptive poet already more than half in love with her image and her letters did Elizabeth Barrett grant audience after he had shown her that he was so sensitive to her wishes that he did not feel free even to walk down Wimpole Street past her door. Not wishing to seem "missish" and a little afraid both of Browning and of his thinking she made much ado about nothing, she let him come one golden afternoon toward the end of May when she feared he talked too loud and stayed too long, hastening that very night to write both his thanks and his fears. Her kindly answer permitting another and yet another Tuesday for their meetings unloosed the bonds of his restraints.

All that the poet had dreamed of he found in this delicate woman who called forth at once his admiration of her intellect, her genius, her wit, and his sympathy for her weakness. From childhood he had poured forth affection on the helpless; and the instinct for protection was now added to his hitherto growing admiration. The actual sight of Elizabeth Barrett inflamed him. He believed her to be an incurable invalid. Her animation contrasted with her physical immobility, her cheerful wit, her wide intellect, her kindliness, her ability to catch and interpret and answer his half spoken thoughts delighted him ever more than her poems; here indeed was a companion god-given. He had never dreamt of such exchange of half-thoughts caught before they were expressed and returned to him in full completeness. In letters she had done just this — she did not find him cryptic! But now to meet her, to see her lovelier than he had dared dream, radiating sweetness and friendliness, understanding him better than he understood himself. . .

With characteristic impetuosity he waited scarcely a day before his feelings mastered him and he wrote the one letter which Elizabeth Barrett dared not keep or even reread. Here was she an invalid, thirty-nine years old; and there was he a splendidly healthy, moderately successful poet of extraordinary promise six years her junior. Could he think she would take advantage of his kindly exuberance of feeling ?   He had mistaken the exquisiteness of his sympathy for love.   Deeply as she was touched — more deeply than she cared to acknowledge even to herself — she could not accept such homage, he a mere boy and she infinitely older and tireder.   He exaggerated the quality of his feeling for her; he was touched by "the humilities" of her position; he was sorry for her, he admired her poetry, and he *thought* he loved her.   It would be unbecoming in her to be vain enough to take him at his word !   He had asked her to read and be silent; he knew he was precipitate but his emotions were too strong for control; speak he must but she need not notice till she knew him better and then he would speak again.   It was a letter to give one joy and pride, were one not so very much older and weaker.   But she must be fair to him.   His friendship was dear to her; she could not give it up; surely he would see reason and would not cease to be her friend because of this one wild letter he would soon want her to forget.   Much troubled of spirit, she wrote him a letter at once perplexed and tender, telling him that he must forget having ever written so wildly, and that he must remain her ever-dear friend and come to see her a week from Tuesday.

Instantly Browning was on his guard.   "I forgot," he wrote, "that one may make too much noise in a silent place by playing the few notes on the 'ear-piercing fife' which in Othello's regimental band might have been thumped into decent subordination by his 'spirit-stirring drum' — to say nothing of gong and ophicleide."   Had she known him better she would not have taken flight at his first honest utterance. In future he would heed better Mephistopheles' advice "never to write a letter, — and never to burn one" ! "Seriously," he concluded, "I am ashamed. . . I shall next ask a servant for my paste in the 'high fantastical' style of my own 'Luria.' "

And so "soundly frightened" he walked softly when next he came to Wimpole Street and let her fuss over his health and exclaim over the beauties of his *Luria* which he was writing as fast as headaches and his absorption in Elizabeth would permit. For having settled the purely friendly nature of their intercourse Elizabeth was now at ease, urging him to come what days he would, and wholly yielding to the delight she found in his company and in his stream of letters. For no sooner did these two see each other and part than they must sit down and write — so many things were left unsaid, so much did each need to interpret himself to the other !

And Elizabeth was like one who should

> Slip slowly down some path worn smooth and even,
> Down to a cool sea on a summer day;
> Yet still in slipping there was some small leaven
>
> Of stretched hands catching small stones by the way,
> Until one surely reached the sea at last . . .

CHAPTER V

HOWEVER refined, love cannot escape its simplest manifestations. Though Elizabeth Barrett did not admit as yet, even to herself, that she was in love, yet like any lovesick girl in her teens she depended wholly upon her lover. The days when he came to see her were golden; soon they came to be the only days she counted. Friends of the past — Miss Mitford, Mr. Kenyon, even hitherto welcome relatives — seemed now an impertinent interruption. How could they know that she wanted all her days free — days when Browning came that his visit might be uninterrupted; days when he did not come that she might be free to write him long and longer letters, to read with minute attention the perfect letters he wrote her; and for the rest to dream on and on ?

Browning himself felt uneasy that she was not writing poetry, feeling guilty lest he should be taking too much of her time with his visits, his letters, and the careful criticism she was giving to his *Duchess* and his *Luria*. Gaily she replied that if indeed her criticisms and emendations were worth anything to him, if he were not mere flatterer, she could contribute more to poesy thus than by composing dozens of poems. Besides she was giving much of her time to getting strong. Nowadays she went out in the carriage and got about the house a little each day.

Browning did not like to think of her thus; she was his recumbent goddess; though he was more than pleased to have her well enough for activity, he had no desire to observe her in any but the graceful posture of her couch.

Meanwhile she tried to stem the tide of her own dreams and desires by casting before him the various obstacles to a union which she had once and for all declared unthinkable. She was much older than he; didn't he know that she had published her *Essay on Mind* in 1826 when he was a mere boy of fourteen ? Age, however, never yet frightened man away; indeed men to whom physical attraction is merely one aspect of love are the more likely to turn to older women, women who offer them in intellectual maturity something not to be found in a miss in her teens. Intellectual companionship meant much to Browning; and in Elizabeth Barrett he found the very complement of his own mind.

Elizabeth tried again, and found that she was a dissenter in religion and hence unsuited to him. This time he laughed outright. Had he not been baptized in the Independent Chapel ? Why she was his sister in the faith !

She began to pray that she might never be "in any way, directly or indirectly, the means of ruffling your smooth path by so much as one of my flint stones !"

Browning was too astute to take direct notice of such naïve confessions of affection; he gloated silently at signatures such as "Ever your E. B. B.," merely hinting at his own feelings more or less cryptically, the clearest being such phrases as: "but as I began, so I shall end"; "my one friend"; "you, my own you past putting away"; and "I will wait."

And so he bode his time. To her he carried his new poems and together they leaned their heads over them, he sure of his strength to refrain from putting hand on her curls; and if hand touched hand in turning the sheets of finely written manuscript, why, that was but chance. She did not recoil from the touch of his fingers; perhaps she did not notice how eager they were. At least she was wise enough to seem not to notice what she might otherwise have had to forbid—and what she did not wish to forbid. Love exacts the same service from low and high. He makes his lovers value physical nearness above all else; and though Elizabeth Barrett and Robert Browning thought they met to discuss poetry they would, had they analysed their conversations, have found that they talked mostly about themselves. So their letters, though sometimes concerned with poetry or criticism, were largely but as the letters of lesser lovers, you and you and you.

Three months from the time that she first saw Robert Browning, from the time when she sternly repressed his love letter, Elizabeth betrayed herself to him unconsciously when, receiving no letter from him for two days, she wrote: "I do not hear; and come to you to ask the alms of one line, having taken it into my head that something is the matter. . . Are you not well—or what? Though I have tried and *wished* to remember having written in the last note something very or even a little offensive to you, I failed in it and go back to the worse fear . . . and if you are not displeased with me, you must

be unwell, I think. . . I am not asking for a letter — but
for a *word* . . . or line strictly speaking."

Now could Browning rightly say that she had given
him "the truest, deepest joy" of his life. Now he could
say to her — though he promised that it should be just
this once until she was ready — "I loved you from my
soul, and gave you my life, so much of it as you would
take, — and all that is *done,* not to be altered now: it
was . . . wholly independent of any return on your
part. . . If I thought you were like other women I have
known . . . but — (my first and last word — I *believe* in
you !) — what you could and would give me of your
affection, you would give nobly and simply and as a
giver — you would not need that I tell you — (*tell* you !)
— what would be supreme happiness to me in the
event — however distant — "

Here in spite of incoherence was something she could
neither misunderstand nor ignore. But after all she was
no impetuous young girl; she could not take him at his
word, she an invalid, six years his senior. Yet her heart
leapt; she let her whole being sing with the joy that swept
over her. To be so loved was to share in paradise. How
glorious to yield, to feel his arms about her, to drink deep
of life's dearest draught ! Her imagination sped forward
into the years, showing what life might be for her . . .
even for her. But she must be generous. She could not
turn aside, however, without one more glance at the possibility of heaven.

At least she could do herself justice; he need not continue to think that she had asked for silence for *her* sake;

surely it could do no harm to let him know that her
motive was pure ? that it was for his sake that she refused
this great gift of his ?   She reminded him that he had
written her long before May that his life had been so full
that he could even afford to risk his happiness.   She could
not feel justified in abetting him in this hazard.   The
love he professed was "a mere generous impulse, likely to
expend itself in a week perhaps."   His persistence moved
her deeply; but perhaps he still mistook the strength of
his love; indeed it would be "more advantageous and
happy" for him if he had so overestimated it.   Though
her intention was entirely to discourage him she could
muster up no stronger argument than this: "Your life !
if you gave it to me and I put my whole heart into it;
what should I put but anxiety, and more sadness than you
were born to ?   What could I give you, which it would
not be ungenerous to give ?   Therefore we must leave
this subject — and I must trust you to leave it without one
word more; (too many have been said already — "

"So, wish by wish, one gets one's wish — at least I do,"
carolled Browning.   He could not wholly restrain his
glee, knowing what she did not, that her barriers were
all but down.   If her heart sang at his letter, his fairly
burst over hers.   For he was a novice in love; he had not
changed his gold coin for a handful of farthings to
scatter here and there; it was fresh and new-minted, all
his to lay at her feet.   All flowers taste more or less alike
to the bee who sips from the garden's richness.   Byron,
gathering his roses by the armful, never knew the perfect
rose.   For Browning now it was blooming; he and he

alone would gather it, if he could but wait and watch, wait and watch.

It is not young love that is thrilling; or rather it is young *love* be the lovers young or old. It is first love that lifts one to the skies and makes one walk on air. And it was truly first and only love that now bound Elizabeth Barrett and Robert Browning. As years went neither was, in common terms, young; in love both were golden lad and lass.

And Browning had felt that this one experience life would not grant him. He had looked forward and charted out his life. He could not know that his immunity would not last; he had wanted love and it had not come; he had not known that it was merely waiting until he was mature enough to grasp its full significance, until he was more worthy . . . But having come it would never depart. Whether or not Elizabeth loved him in return, his love would never waver. Here was for him life's unalterable reality.

"Dearest, I will end here — words, persuasion, arguments, if they were at my service I would not use them — I believe in you, altogether have faith in you — in you . . . I look on and on over the prospect of my love, it is all *on*wards — and all possible forms of unkindness . . . I quite laugh to think how they are *behind* . . . cannot be encountered in the route we are travelling ! . . . I am yours —

"Yes, Yours ever. God bless you for all you have been, and are, and will certainly be to me, come what He shall please !"

How hard he made matters for her ! For she knew now how dearly she loved him, how much it would mean to her to say a simple yes, and start life afresh with this counterpart of her very mind and soul. Sadly she told him how no man had ever before meant anything to her, how if she were but "different in some respects and free in others . . ." she would accept the great gift of his happiness, "gladly, proudly, and gratefully; and give away my own life and soul to that end. I *would* do it . . . *not, I do* . . . observe ! . . . I am not likely to help you in wrong against yourself."

Though this presumably ended the matter she could not refrain from urging her father's implacable objections to the marriage of his children; and then swerving to the other side of the argument unconsciously, she stated that Browning's generous intent to take up a lucrative position would have been unnecessary — and she could not bear it — because she had an ample income quite her own.

"I will wait, I will wait," became the burden of Browning's letters, but his eyes spoke more ardently when he leaned over her hand, when he looked long and earnestly at her during his visits. Quite visibly he was restraining himself, voice and hand. Elizabeth no longer had the ability to separate this handsome man from the man of her letters. For a long time they had been to her two people; this Browning, genuine poet, man about town, who came once a week to share his sunshine with his fellow craftsman; and that other Browning to whom she poured out her feelings and who caught them and sent them back to her glorified. This Browning of the letters was from the first an extension of herself. The real Browning who sat beside her and patted Flush while they discussed literature and art had been a bit awe-inspiring for all his kindness. Now that his words vibrated with feeling, now that he let slip endearing phrases which she dared neither notice nor reprove, he was one with himself and with her.

Her perplexities found expression in *A Denial:*

I

We have met late — it is too late to meet,
   O friend, not more than friend!
Death's forecome shroud is tangled round my feet,
And if I step or stir, I touch the end.
   In this last jeopardy
Can I approach thee I, who cannot move ?
How shall I answer thy request for love ?
   Look in my face and see.

II

I love thee not, I dare not love thee ! go
   In silence; drop my hand.
If thou seek roses, seek them where they blow
In garden-alleys, not in desert-sand.
   Can life and death agree,
That thou shouldst stoop thy song to my complaint ?
I cannot love thee. If the word is faint,
   "Look in my face and see."

III

I might have loved thee in some former days.
   Oh, then, my spirits had leapt
As now they sink, at hearing thy love-praise.
Before these faded cheeks were overwept,

Had this been asked of me,
To love thee with my whole strong heart and head, —
I should have said still . . . yes, but *smiled* and said,
"Look in my face and see !"

IV

But now . . . God sees me, God, who took my heart
   And drowned it in life's surge.
In all your wide warm earth I have no part —
A light song overcomes me like a dirge.
   Could love's great harmony
The saints keep step to when their bonds are loose,
Not weigh me down ? am *I* a wife to choose ?
   Look in my face and see.

V

While I behold, as plain as one who dreams,
   Some woman of full worth,
Whose voice, as cadenced as a silver stream's,
Shall prove the fountain-soul which sends it forth;
   One younger, more thought-free
And fair and gay, than I, thou must forget,
With brighter eyes than these . . . which are not wet . . .
   Look in my face and see.

VI

So farewell thou, whom I have known too late
   To let thee come so near.
Be counted happy while men call thee great,
And one belovèd woman feels thee dear ! —
   Not I ! — that cannot be.
I am lost, I am changed, — I must go farther, where
The change shall take me worse, and no one dare
   Look in my face to see.

VII

Meantime I bless thee. By these thoughts of mine
   I bless thee from all such !
I bless thy lamp to oil, thy cup to wine,
Thy hearth to joy, thy hand to an equal touch
   Of loyal troth. For me
I love thee not, I love thee not ! — away !
Here's no more courage in my soul to say
   "Look in my face and see."

Knowing at last her lack of strength, her inability to resist, nay her inability to refuse herself this great happiness, she capitulated completely. She yielded to her own desire and wrote: "Henceforward I am yours for everything but to do you harm — and I am yours too much, in my heart, ever to consent to do you harm in that way. If I could consent to do it, not only should I be less loyal . . . but in one sense, less yours . . . none, except God and your will, shall interpose between you and me . . . I mean, that if He should free me within a moderate time from the trailing chain of this weakness, I will then be to you whatever at that hour you shall choose . . . whether friend or more than friend . . . a friend to the last in any case. So it rests with God and with you — only in the meanwhile you are most absolutely free . . . 'unentangled' (as they call it) by the breadth of a thread —"

"Oh," sang Browning's instant reply, "do not fear I am *'entangled'* — my crown is loose on my head, not nailed there — my pearl lies in my hand — I may return it to the sea, if I will !"

But he was not precipitate; sure now of her love as he

was of his own for her he was content to walk softly savoring the scent of each blossom until finally he should hold in his hand the full harvest of the garden.   This love of his was his whole life's emotion; he could afford to wait for completion taking her with him step by step until together they "surely reached the sea at last."

Besides, there were very real obstacles.   Even if her health mended to the point where she would feel that she was not imposing upon his generosity by giving him an invalid for wife, and he would feel that in taking her he did not risk her very existence, there was still the wall of Mr. Barrett's prohibition.   Not that he was consulted. His children had long since learned what matters could best be carried on without his knowledge.   So long as he was not openly crossed he was a fairly genial and decidedly indulgent parent.   To Elizabeth's room he brought armfuls of reading matter carefully selected to give her pleasure.   He would surprise and delight his family by the purchase of some art treasure, — an Andrea del Sarto hung above the mantelpiece, about which the family would cluster with excited comment, until some one — gentle, kindly, devoted Arabel, perhaps — would remember Elizabeth shut away upstairs unable to share their pleasure.   Then up the stairs would dash Stormie or George, laughingly seize the startled sister, and carry her with terrifying speed down the stairs, into the drawing-room, to toss her triumphantly on the sofa and bid her look.

Mr. Barrett was, in truth, no inhuman monster.   He had taste and wit and a fund of good humor.   Something in his life or in his religion had warped him. His domination over his children was not especially remarkable at a time when the heavy-handed father was no rare specimen. But his lack of hospitality — even Mr. Kenyon could never be asked to dinner — was certainly un-English, and his absolute abhorrence of marriage was psychopathic. He never stated his reasons; he merely flatly refused consent to sons and daughters when occasion arose: the match was not suitable.

Of Elizabeth he was naturally not suspicious. He took pride in her genius; he enjoyed her success; but he had something of contempt for her weak physical state. He pampered her, he let her have a steady procession of doctors; with amused tolerance he watched her fed drugs, drugs to strengthen her pulse, drugs to put her to sleep, all the time feeling that hers was a womanish complaint born of too much languor and too little red meat. She was not one to attract men; she would not get entangled like the foolish Henrietta. Besides, this notion of hers not to see people, to stay shut up in her room kept her from contact with men. She was safe, this treasure of his, safe as a little saint in her shrine.

For undoubtedly, part of Mr. Barrett's objection to marriage was his dislike of parting his enormous family. He liked to dwell like a patriarch among his fold; his community must be held together. He had let two of the boys get their university education in Glasgow; he had let Elizabeth go to Torquay — and as she could never go by herself this had meant losing Arabel, too; and then she had demanded Edward, with what a result! He let the other girls visit friends from time to time; he let the boys go to the continent; he even let two of them sail for strange lands in the vessels he loved to buy for speculation. It was perhaps good for young people to leave home now and then and see for themselves how hard the world could be. Boys who had suffered thirst and hunger and cold (though this had been unforeseen accident) on a long voyage would be content at home for a while. On the whole his little kingdom was not hard to rule; his subjects were well in hand.

So he could sip Elizabeth's cherished Cyprus wine, given with royal generosity by Mr. Boyd, and call it a nauseous draught. He could stop to chat now and then with Mr. Kenyon or undaunted Miss Mitford, who would gossip gaily or ride intrepid over his known prejudices. Except for a handful of incense-burning females and a few relatives or old neighbors who occasionally came to town, these were all Elizabeth's visitors. Nothing to fear from Kenyon! His courtly manners, his ready wit, his polished conversation could never romanticize his ruddy countenance, his huge bulk. One could as well pair a humming bird and a bear!

Mr. Barrett did not long remain unaware of Robert Browning's visits; and he managed to slip home early to meet the poet during one of his afternoons with Elizabeth. Nothing to fear here, he thought. This robust young man, quite a man about town, could have no amorous designs. They talked of poetry, these two, reading each other the poem of the moment, discussing critical standards and the works of their contemporaries.

Doubtless he was moved partly by generosity toward the frail poetess chained to her couch. Let him come, if he amused her. In his blindness Mr. Barrett chaffed Elizabeth a little about her new admirer; and then went on his way serene that all was well within his stronghold.

It was therefore not necessary for Elizabeth to falsify, merely to keep quiet. Her brothers teased her, being slightly suspicious of such a constant friend, but neither they nor her more penetrating sisters would betray her. Henrietta, too, was safe from their spying though Captain Cook sat in the parlor day after day weeping and wooing and breaking down her soft resistance by sheer force of his presence. Neither spies nor informers were the Barretts. Had Elizabeth been less timid she could have received Robert Browning daily; but so great was her fear that something would happen to wreck her happiness in his love that she dared not let him come regularly more than once a week — though twice a week came to be not unusual. Three times in two weeks was, in general, the most she dared permit, lest her father becoming suspicious should shower wrath upon her or utter a prohibition. She had gone contrary to his wishes once and had lost him a son, and herself the being she had most loved. Now she loved again, a love beside which her affection for her brother seemed pale. She could not risk the faintest shadow of that devastating disapproval. Appeal to her father she knew to be utterly vain. Browning thought that a direct application might move him. "You might," declared Elizabeth, "as well think to sweep off a third of the stars of Heaven with the motion of your eyelashes !"

With such an opinion of her father and with such memories of his disapproval, it is small wonder that she temporized. Moreover she was constantly taking laudanum — forty drops a day — without which, she was assured by her doctor, her heart faltered; and she knew she could not sleep. That, too, contributed to her lack of definiteness. She could not lessen her dose even at Browning's plea, he fearing the effects of the drug especially now that her health was of such moment, when upon the chance of her improved health was cast the die of their marriage.

For that health she was prepared to make heroic struggles. Long since the doctors had pronounced London winters too harsh for her and had prescribed a milder climate: Malta, Madeira, Italy. Plans had been under way for her wintering in Italy this year. She was eagerly interested, believing that if she could successfully withstand the winter she would not be wholly rash in marrying; she would not be imposing upon her lover the burden of a completely invalided wife. It was never a matter of money; her present income of some four hundred pounds could easily be increased, perhaps doubled by careful reinvestment; she was free to go where she would if her father but gave permission.

It is not strange that she thought that permission necessary. For one thing she had led an oddly sheltered life, even in the days of protected womanhood. And in her few journeyings and outings she had never been alone or alone with a maid. Wherever she moved there also went a sister and a brother as a sort of bodyguard. So now that she meditated Italy she felt that she could not go without at least one brother as courier and one sister as companion.

Mr. Barrett, then, was called upon to lose from his family circle three of his children. Two daughters, one of them perfectly well and able to mix in society, and one son would be transported to a different country quite beyond his authority and influence. He honestly did not believe that this separation from him, the font and origin of their lives, their guide, mentor, and legal code, was wise for them. If Elizabeth had to be vaporish, she could manage comfortably at home; doctors could bend as solicitously over her here as there. She was doing very well; she wrote first-rate poetry; a little less coddling of herself, a little more will, and she would live sensibly like her sisters. Families needed to hold together. He had let Elizabeth have her way once, that time in Torquay . . . this trip to Italy might prove just such another tragedy. Perverse creatures, women. What was to be gained by this journey ? He would be three children the poorer; they, without him to watch over them, would be the foolisher. Enough of this affair of Pisa. Elizabeth was more comfortable in her own home. If she could not get out of bed here, why should she be any better there ? It was not a matter of climate; it was a matter of will power and common sense. Let her eat like other people, drink good strong ale and fine old port instead of that nauseous Greek wine, and she'd recover from these fainting spells.

He could not be unaware of the undercurrent of treachery in his household. Naturally a holiday in Pisa sounded attractive to Arabel and Stormie; they would plot with Elizabeth to outwit him. He was sufficiently disturbed to omit for a time his nightly visits to his daughter's room; he had been in the habit of going to her when he returned at night at eleven or twelve and talking with her a while; and then, sharing with her his nightly devotions, he would kneel beside her bed and pray. He could not do this while her thoughts were disloyal to him. He could not let her think she was free of his displeasure.

Meanwhile Elizabeth hoped and feared, yet neither wholeheartedly. If she went she would obviously have to face her father's displeasure in spite of his relenting (as surely he must for her health's sake if he cared for her); and that would be grievous; worse still she would have to part with Robert Browning, miss his dear visits, fail for a time to receive his letters, visits and letters which were more than life to her.

He would follow her to Pisa, or to the ends of the earth, so he said, so she knew; there was no longer doubt of him or doubt of herself; but separation would be inevitable for a time; and that separation she could not easily face. She could still say: "I am yours, your own — only not to *hurt you*"; in the face of his breathless letters she knew that even that reservation would go — and yet the miracle of his love was almost incredible. "I have sometimes," she wrote, "felt jealous of myself . . . of my own infirmities . . . and thought that you cared for me only because your chivalry touched them with a silver sound — and that, without them, you would pass by on the other side: — why twenty times I have thought *that* and been vexed — ungrateful vexation !"

Romantic Elizabeth in her youth when other young ladies discussing their prince charmings of the future had demanded this or that virtue, this or that reason for loving and being loved, had vehemently declared that *if* she were ever loved she would want her prince to love her "just because." He who could pour forth all his emotion on "an idiot with a goitre" for no reason but that he *loved* her, why he loved truly. She remembered how her friends had laughed at her. And here was her great poet come wooing *her,* weak pallid creature, and he answered her as she would have had him; no chivalry his; he loved because he loved, and that was all; not her weakness, not her talent for scribbling rhymes; just herself he loved.

To her he wrote: "My life is bound up with yours — my own, first and last love . . . And it seems strange to me how little — less than little I have laid open of my feelings, the nature of them to you . . . I have not said . . . what I will not even now say . . . you will *know* — in God's time to which I trust." And again: "I do believe that we shall be happy; . . . you see I can confidently expect *the* end to it all . . . so it has always been with me in my life of wonders — absolute wonders, with God's hand over all . . . And this last and best of all would never have begun so, and gone on so, to break off abruptly even here, in the world, for the little time.

". . . Why we shall see Italy together !   I could, would, *will* shut myself in four walls of a room with you and never leave you and be most of all *then* 'a lord of infinite space' — but, to travel with you to Italy, or Greece. . ."

Her cup ran over. "And now how am I to feel when you tell me what you have told me; and what you 'could would and will' do, and *shall not* do ?"   She could only wrap herself in these intoxicating dreams, dreams of life in love, dreams rosier than any of girl in teens, because she was in full mental vigor, emotionally ripe after a singularly secluded life even as Browning, after a busily social life constantly but vainly hitherto exposed to love.   She could but write that, dramatic poet though he was, he could not fathom the full depth of his meaning to her, he an angel at her prison gate: "My wonder is greater than your wonders, I who sat here alone but yesterday, so weary of my own being that to take interest in my very poems I had to lift them up by an effort and separate them from myself and cast them out from me into the sunshine where I was not — feeling nothing of the light which fell on them even — making indeed a sort of pleasure and interest about that factitious personality associated with them . . . but knowing it to be all far on the outside of *me* . . . *myself* . . . not seeming to touch it with the end of my finger . . . and receiving it as a mockery and a bitterness when people persisted in confounding one with another.   Morbid it was if you like it — perhaps very morbid — but all these heaps of letters which go into the fire one after the other, and which, because I am a woman and have written verses, it seems so amusing to the letter-writers of your sex to write and see 'what will come of it,' . . . some, from kind good motives I know, . . . well, . . . how could it all make for me even such a narrow strip of sunshine as Flush finds on the floor sometimes, and lays his nose along, with both ears out in the shadow ? It was not for *me* . . . *me* . . . in any way: it was not within my reach — I did not seem to touch it, as I said. Flush came nearer, and I was grateful to him . . . yes grateful . . . for not being tired ! I have felt grateful and flattered . . . yes flattered . . . when he has chosen rather to stay with me all day than go downstairs. Grateful too, with reason, I have been and am to my own family for not letting me see that I was a burthen."

In such a humble spirit did she accept Browning's devotion, insisting that nevertheless he must be perfectly free, since already she was "too rich by you, to claim any debt."

Freedom was neither to Browning's liking nor was it even possible. "I am not conscious," he wrote, "of thinking or feeling but *about* you . . . so I will live, so may I die !"

Their interviews were not frequent enough or long enough to satisfy either of them. Their love cycle had to run largely on the limitless track of pen and paper. "When I come back from seeing you," wrote Browning, "and think over it all, there never is a least word of yours I could not occupy myself with, and wish to return to

you with some . . . not to say, all . . . the thoughts
and fancies it is sure to call out of me. You possess me,
dearest . . . and there is no help for the expressing it all,
no voice nor hand, but these of mine which shrink and
turn away from the attempt."

He would bring her flowers which she would forget
until he was gone when she would herself rise to put
them in water; and they would have the grace to survive
even when he, all unheeding, had sat upon them for up-
wards of two hours ! It was a good omen that his flowers
lived with her in her room where other flowers had
always died. Pure magic this was, not the fact that these
were always the freshest of flowers, and tenderly cared
for, their stems meticulously clipt, their water constantly
renewed. While she tended them Elizabeth would let
her thoughts stray fancy free toward this promised land
of love: "and while I was putting them into the water
I thought that your visit went on all the time. . . To say
now that I never can forget; that I feel bound to you
as one human being cannot be more bound to another,
and that you are more to me at this moment than all the
rest of the world, is only to say in new words that it
would be a wrong against *myself,* to seem to risk your
happiness and abuse your generosity."

She knew now that she was not to go to Italy. Her
brother George as her advocate had had a stormy session
with Mr. Barrett. Passion ran high in the Barrett family;
such scenes were dramatic and terrible. Elizabeth cow-
ered in her distant chamber while voices rose and rose.
The heavy tramping of feet, the pitiless thunder of words

penetrated her trembling seclusion though she could not make out the actual terms of their discourse. She knew the storm had broken; she sensed rather than actually heard its roar. Was anything in the world — much less a mere trip to Italy, even the regaining of health, worth this dreadful upheaval, this loss of decent dignity, this absolute destruction of the dam of reserve which now the torrent of recrimination tore ? Only her love of Browning, her desire to make herself well for him, — for her own happiness she would not have risked this, would not so have exposed her brother, would not even so have distressed her father; but convinced that Browning's happiness was bound up with her health, she would — almost — have dared herself face her father with the request that was bringing down upon George's unoffending head blow upon blow of fierce invective.

This insanity of rage she could understand, too; as a child she had shown its inherited effects; she, too, had kicked and screamed, beaten senseless tables and broken chairs. She remembered now how she had actually *enjoyed* her rages, sometimes not even having the grace to be ashamed of them in the calm afterwards. So she felt her father enjoyed his rages; he was actually loosening the bonds of decency, of civilization; he was yielding without restraint to primitive impulses. Perhaps he, too, would repent as she used to as she grew older and more responsible, repent and try to heal the bruises she had made on furniture and friends. He had been frighteningly angry when she detained Edward at Torquay; frightfully bitter — nay, almost vindictive; but he had forgiven her after Edward's death; had forgiven her and had been kinder and more indulgent, trying to bring her out of her lethargy and making her feel that somehow she was extraordinarily dear to him. All she asked now was a chance to regain health . . . but was that really all she asked? Was she not asking him to let her go temporarily that she might completely disobey him and go forever? But he did not know, he could not suspect. If he loved her he would welcome this experiment of a winter in Italy's soft climate; he would want her to be rid of this heavy invalidism. Resolutely she shut her mind to the reality of her treachery; she was making a reasonable request; if he denied it she could not doubt that his love for her was imaginary, a figment of her own gentle imagination. And then there would creep into her consciousness the knowledge that after all she would be not wholly glad to go, since going meant a temporary loss of Browning's dear companionship, and further a change in the status quo of their relationship. The present moment was so beautiful — could they but detain it would not life be perfect?

George's step was on the stairs. She did not need to hear him speak; one look at his distressed face and she knew her fate. She was not to go. All his pleading, his lawyer's arguing, his man's loss of temper had gained for her was her father's permission to go if she *pleased, under his heaviest displeasure,* however; and if she went, he was "through with her." Just where her duty now lay was somewhat uncertain. Her father would not discuss the matter with her even if she could grasp her courage in two hands and face him with it.   George had done his utmost and failed.   There was no use in appeal.   Either she would go and be unforgiven or she would remain until such time as she could face flight with Browning.   She thought that she decided to stay both because she shrank from her father's wrath and because she refused to be selfish and involve her sister and brother in her downfall.   She had never thought of going alone; if she went Arabel and Stormie were necessary to her.   They were both willing to go — perhaps eager to go after their father's ultimatum.   The responsibility of taking them thus seemed to Elizabeth too heavy.

She nursed her disappointment and her disillusionment; she had thought her father loved her beyond the common measure; she could no longer believe that he loved her at all.   She turned the more to Browning of whose love she was indeed sure.   And quite unbidden there sprang up in her heart a feeling of joy.   They would not need to be separated after all.   There would be for the long present no readjustment.   Under other skies, he might not love her quite so much.   No blame to him !   Still — the fly in the ointment — he had planned on winter in Italy; ought she to deprive him of his holiday because she was not to have hers ?   The parting perhaps must come after all; she must be brave; she would have his letters; he would come back — and if he did not, her cup was already full and running over.   "I am happy enough to die now," she wrote.   And he could go to Italy and be rid of the headaches that wracked him in England.

Go to Italy without her ? he retorted.   The grace of

her "imaginary self-denial" was none of his. "I love you," he answered, "because I love you; I see you 'once a week' because I cannot see you all day long; I think of you all day long, because I most certainly could not think of you once an hour less, if I tried, or went to Pisa. . . Do you really think that before I found you, I was going about the world seeking whom I might devour, that is, be devoured by, in the shape of a wife . . . do you suppose I ever dreamed of marrying ?"

Thus day by day he hammered upon the wall of her resistance, even he not half suspecting its weakness — and though he filled page after page, though he poured lengthy letter and lyric note upon her, mere prose could not suffice him. "You throw largesses out on all sides without counting the coins," wrote Elizabeth when she read the manuscript he submitted to her for her comments and revisions. *"Love me forever"* ran the refrain of his poems; who was she to resist the current of his mighty river ?

Nay but you, who do not love her,
　Is she not pure gold, my mistress ?
Holds earth aught — speak truth — above her ?
　Aught like this tress, see, and this tress,
And this last fairest tress of all,
So fair, see, ere I let it fall ?

Because you spend your lives in praising;
　To praise, you search the wide world over:
Then why not witness, calmly gazing,
　If earth holds aught — speak truth — above her ?
Above this tress, and this, I touch
But cannot praise, I love so much !

CHAPTER VI

B UT BROWNING was no ascetic lover. He was not one to be content with holding his lady's hand and gazing into her fair eyes. He could not, like Captain Surtees Cook who sat in the parlor with Henrietta dumbly hoping and never daring, be content with an insufficient present, an indefinite future. He was neither rash nor precipitate; having waited long for love, having believed himself immune (even a little proud of his immunity) he was not sorry to tread holy ground softly and slowly. The present held much, nay, more than he could wholly grasp in one handful; there was need of time for them both fully to realize the wonder that was theirs. He was content as she was to wade step by step into that deep and permanent intimacy toward which he at least had set his face from the very beginning. It was delicious to gain intimacy bit by bit; first the letters, then the interviews, then both letters and interviews and the creeping in of soft endearments; he numbered the letters, he counted the minutes of their being together — he proudly recorded that now those precious hours had mounted up to twenty-four, one whole day of life and love; he begged and gained the gift of a lock of hair; he wrote: "I want ALL of you, not just so much as I could not live without." This was no timid lover, like Henrietta's.

If Elizabeth had any doubts as to the nature of affection his behavior soon dispelled them. At first to avoid awkwardness, their actual interviews had remained much as before. They discussed poetry and poetic theory; he brought her his new poems and read them to her; he recounted his progress with his new and last drama for *Bells and Pomegranates,* his "darling Luria"; and then he went home to write what he dared not speak. Gradually little loving words would escape him, words which she tried to disregard until for all her watchfulness she found herself using them, too. She knew she ought to say him nay; she tried and failed. Her mind — no, her conscience, said no; her heart said yes. When he first kissed her hand it was doubtful which of the two was the more embarrassed. They were both novices in the art of loving; they had to learn step by step this path of love; they sipped their heady wine, savoring each drop.

> First time he kissed me, he but only kissed
> The fingers of this hand wherewith I write;
> And, ever since, it grew more clean and white . . .
> . . . A ring of amethyst
> I could not wear here, plainer to my sight,
> Than that first kiss. The second passed in height
> The first, and sought the forehead, and half missed,
> Half falling on the hair. Oh, beyond meed!
> That was the chrism of love, which love's own
>   crown,
> With sanctifying sweetness, did precede.
> The third upon my lips was folded down
> In perfect, purple state; since when, indeed,
> I have been proud and said, "My love, my own."

There was no swift step from hand to lips; Browning had need to be gentle and slow both because of the fullness of his heart and the shyness of Elizabeth. She was, she confessed, living in a dream, "leaning half out of some turret-window of the Castle of Indolence and watching the new sunrise," dazzled by its glory. By her very reverence for Browning's genius she felt the impossibility of this dream, the almost certainty that she was self-deceived. "What was *I*," she wrote, "that I should think otherwise ? I had been shut up here too long face to face with my own spirit, not to know myself, and so, to have lost the common illusions of vanity . . . *Can* it be, I say to myself, that *you* feel for me *so* ? can it be meant for me ? this from *you* ?"

And yet he called her his love, his "own, best, extreme life's end"; he wrote that he "was made and meant to look for you and wait for you and become your own forever"; and again: "And now my love . . . my whole life is wound up and down and over you. . ." He had come into her desert and lo, it became a grove of palm trees.

Still, complete surrender was not now. She knew her shyness was part prudery; in time, perhaps — And so a great to-do had to be made over his request (by letter; he had not the courage face to face !) for a lock of her hair which she granted half laughing at her own reluctance, provided it be a fair exchange. Even then the giving was not simple. She cut two locks which for want of a skein of silk to tie them got wofully tangled, whereupon losing her patience and temper — and the post — she came near denuding her head and casting all her hair into the fire with the two offending locks. At the critical moment Wilson produced the silk, the lock was conveyed to a jeweller, and a ring, blue as the flowers Browning brought her, was chosen to hold the hair. This gift he might not mention when he saw her; while his she tucked into a locket once given her by an uncle, who had warned her to beware of loving, she who if she loved would love beyond measure. He might not mention her gift; he must merely take it with a promise implied: "If ever you care less for me — I do not say it in distrust of you . . . I trust you wholly — but you are a man, and free to care less . . . and if you ever *do* . . . why in that case you will destroy, burn . . . do all but send back — "

Now for all his love Browning could not refrain from gentle teasing. He agreed at once, not even, so he wrote gaily, making his promise conditional upon her promise to see that in that case they care for him properly at the insane asylum !

She could not escape teasing in spite of her caution in avoiding mention of Browning, skilfully fencing as she did with Miss Mitford, with Mr. Kenyon, with the handful of admiring literary ladies who now and then called upon her, cunningly guiding the conversation around the corner when she saw Browning's name about to appear on a signpost. Mr. Kenyon was hardest to evade. He *would* drag Browning into the conversation, asking her opinion on his poems and on the reviews which praised or blamed them. It was hard to be composed and unblushing under his keen eyes. Once he came triumphantly bearing copies of manuscript verses of Browning's, having been allowed by Browning's sister to see and copy them before they went to print. He read them to her and asked her comment. Strongly tempted by her familiar devil not to say she had read them before, she "spoke the truth and shamed the devil and surprised Mr. Kenyon" who said nothing for the moment, being indeed, somewhat taken back by what must mean something of an intimacy between this cousin of his and Robert Browning, an intimacy of which he had not had an inkling. Half an hour later as he prepared to depart Mr. Kenyon asked her drily how long ago she had heard these poems. He was constantly embarrassing her with questions; he would ask how often she saw Browning, knowing that she had refused to see Horne and even Wordsworth's great self — at least he had refused Wordsworth for her, and she had so temporized and hemmed and hawed and been uncertain that Horne had finally paid her out in her own coin and trotted off to Germany unseen. Mr. Kenyon, not knowing how much she had to conceal, would suggest that Browning stop at his door on the days he visited Elizabeth; why could he not stop to dinner with Kenyon?

Somewhat heartier was the teasing of her brothers. From them she felt it wise to conceal Browning's gift of a ring no less than his lock of hair. Were they to remark either they would besiege her with "questions 'how' . . . 'what' . . . 'why' . . . put round and edgeways"; they would badger her until she would with an assumption of calmness answer, "Well: how many more

questions ?"   Her timidity in removing Browning's portrait the day she had first received him had not gone
unnoticed though she had at the same time — out of
justice, she said — taken down Tennyson, leaving Wordsworth and Carlyle to keep company with Harriet Martineau.   Her brothers would prance about her room opening boxes and drawers to scatter their contents roughly
about, rudely commenting on her feminine fripperies,
until at last they unearthed the two poet-heads to hang
on their old nails; while they discoursed loud and long
on the virtues of their verses and the points of their
physiognomies.   Not satisfied, they would go on to ana-
lyse what they called her "absurdity" in removing the
pictures.   At first she would, after preserving an obstinate
silence during their gay performance, have the pictures
removed and concealed in some new hiding place.   Her
brothers, however, were too persistent in their searches
to give her peace.   To end their horseplay she finally fas-
tened Browning's picture firmly inside a copy of *Para-
celsus* where it remained, this time safely hidden.

George, the lawyer brother, time and again met Browning at the dinner table of Kenyon or other friends and
pleased Elizabeth by choosing to like him.   With Browning he had his fun silently, gravely answering polite
inquiries for Miss Barrett's health as if he did not know
that the information he gave was quite superfluous.   He
enjoyed Browning's embarrassed queries, knowing that
the poet, having been with Elizabeth all afternoon, was
more aware of the state of her health than her brother.
Such vexations were purely minor ripples in their hap-

piness. "Why what nonsense we have come to — we who ought to be talking Greek !" she wrote after a very farrago of fond lovers' talk. Yet it was not all gaiety in spite of the weather which mistook November for April, leaving her strength unimpaired; there was the great fear that she was not being fair to him, not worthy of his superlatives when he called her "the direct miraculous gift of God." He was that to her, he who was all that was great and good and kind.

In her humility she thought again and again that it were perhaps best if she should die this winter before she had disappointed him in anything. "When you come to know me as well as I know myself, what can save me, do you think, from disappointing and displeasing you ?" Only her deep love must speak for her, only that could keep her alive for him.

Browning's task it was to teach her that this communication of theirs, daily, twice daily, with interviews strung like beads upon a chain, was not enough. Fearing to frighten her he kept himself in check when he saw her, until such time as she should become accustomed to his passionate outpourings through his letters. He wrote: "And love, all love is but a passionate *drawing closer* — I would be one with you, dearest; let my soul press close to you, as my lips, dear life of my life." When he heard how well she was — in spite of winter's coming — able still to be about and walk he said: "Shall I not know one day how far your mouth will be from mine as we walk ?"

The contrast between his ardent letters and the conventional coolness of his visits could not last. Shyly she indicated their discrepancy, the difference she felt between the writing and the speaking man; at once Browning cast restraint aside. Kisses rained on lips and eyes; now was she sealed and stamped with his love. The intoxication of those kisses — the first he had given or taken in love — sent Browning off to work furiously on his beloved *Luria* more golden than ever in the reflected light of passion. He wrote that he might have new laurels to lay at his lady's feet; he wrote because somehow he must express the surging tide of his emotions. And he would pause in his poetry to write and write and write again how much he loved her, how impossible were life without her. "We are to live together one day, love !" she read and thrilled to the melody of his one note. She might retort: "You exaggerate, sir !" but by the depth and range of her own feeling for him she knew that he did not. She might tease him a little perhaps just for the sake of his dear answers: "And it is *not* foolish in me to love the table and chairs and vases in your room !"

Though he had not yet seen her on her feet, he knew that she did stand and walk. The winter, unusually mild and springlike, encouraged her to effort. The constant joy of Browning's love rejuvenated her until her sisters jestingly remarked that she was but playing invalid and soon would lose the faintest excuse for being one. Seeing her thus gain strength where in previous years she had lost it, Browning grew bold. "But this living without you is tormenting now. So begin thinking as for a new year, as for a new life."

He wrote:

So, I shall see her in three days
And just one night, but nights are short,
Then two long hours, and that is morn.
See how I come, unchanged, unworn !
Feel, where my life broke off from thine,
How fresh the splinters keep and fine, —
Only a touch and we combine!

Too long, this time of year, the days !
But nights, at least the nights are short.
As night shows where her one moon is,
A hand's-breadth of pure light and bliss,
So life's night gives my lady birth
And my eyes hold her !   What is worth
The rest of heaven, the rest of earth ?

O loaded curls, release your store
Of warmth and scent, as once before
The tingling hair did, lights and darks
Outbreaking into fairy sparks,
When under curl and curl I pried
After the warmth and scent inside,
Through lights and darks how manifold —
The dark inspired, the light controlled !
As early Art embrowns the gold.

What great fear, should one say, "Three days
That change the world might change as well
Your fortune; and if joy delays,
Be happy that no worse befell !"
What small fear, if another says,

"Three days and one short night beside
May throw no shadow on your ways;
But years must teem with change untried,
With chance not easily defied,
With an end somewhere undescried."
No fear ! — or if a fear be born
This minute, it dies out in scorn.
Fear ! I shall see her in three days
And one night, now the nights are short,
Then just two hours, and that is morn.

So hard was it for them both now to be cicumspect, so hard to wait through the days between Monday and Saturday, between Saturday and Tuesday, that all Elizabeth's *if's* became *when's*. With this new health of hers she no longer needed to discipline herself, to threaten herself with the crucifixion of losing her lover. She could, without feeling herself a traitor to his good, yield to his insistence upon marriage at the summer's end.

Summer's end seemed so far away to their impatience that on the days when they did not meet they time and again became despondent. Yet surely the fates were with them, even when tempted by a bit of foolish questioning. Thinking of Elizabeth as he studied far off in his room, Browning had a fancy to try the lots with a book. Asking what would be "the event of my love for Her" he seized upon the first book that came to his hand, finding it to his consternation to be nothing but an Italian grammar, sure to prove sterile. Nevertheless it was necessary for the laws of chance that he abide by his choice. He opened the book at random — and fell upon this, from the "Promiscuous Exercises" to be translated into Italian:

"If we love in the other world as we do in this, I shall love thee to eternity !"

And thus the stream of their love moved on toward fulfilment, the indefinite "some time" gradually becoming a not wholly definite autumn time, with just enough whirlpools to make the journey exciting. She worried over his headaches, he over her opium — she had taken morphine steadily though not in increasing doses; now at his request she began to lessen the dose slowly as seemed safest. Then there were the dangers of detection. Shrewd Mr. Kenyon had his suspicions, increased by her halting refusals to show him Browning's letters as she had those of other admirers. Her sisters were entirely in the secret and both sympathetic. From Browning's family there was nothing to fear — his sister constantly sent Elizabeth flowers; and with his mother and his father he was on such understanding terms that they were happy in his happiness. Elizabeth's brothers saw too little of her to be wholly aware. They knew of Browning's visits, they managed to catch glimpses of him, and they thought her rather partial to her poet-friend. To confide in them would, Elizabeth felt, be unfair since they would then be involved in her father's wrath. Of that she was perfectly sure. To Browning's request that he be allowed to try his luck with Mr. Barrett Elizabeth shuddered. "He would rather see me dead at his foot," she insisted, "and he will say so, and mean it, and persist in the meaning."

Though unsuspicious of Elizabeth Mr. Barrett could not be ignorant of Captain Surtees Cook's persistent adoration of Henrietta. Sure, however, that Henrietta after her previous experience of his anger would not dare to cross him were Captain Cook forever to remain languishing, Mr. Barrett rather liked the captain. He almost included him in the family, so used did he become to finding him in the drawing-room. One day, feeling somehow the undercurrent of disobedience in his children's attitude, Mr. Barrett burst into a sermon on filial obedience. "Passive obedience" was his creed; and in nothing was this more necessary than in the matter of marriage. One by one his numerous sons rose quietly and left the room leaving for sole auditor the lovesick captain, who at the end of the tirade had just spirit enough to ask meekly "if children were to be considered slaves."

And though Mr. Barrett stuck obstinately to his patriarchal system, hypnotizing himself into the belief that it was successfully in force with his family, he could not be wholly unaware of the isolation in which he lived. His children were his — on the surface. Beyond that they had no manner of converse with him. Outwardly they conformed; and with that outward conformity he had to seem satisfied. Sometimes he became aware of his isolation, of the cold silence in which he lived. He would punish his children by withdrawing still further from them and believe them pained by his withdrawal.

Rather did they shrug their shoulders and go about their own lives, striving to make them touch his at as few points as possible. For Elizabeth the result of her father's fixed attitude was the determination not even to seek his consent. She could and would do without it. Once she would have tried with all her wiles, with all her heart and soul, to win him over to her way of thinking — or at least she would not have knowingly run in direct opposition to him. Now, wrapt wholly in her love for Browning, she felt no longer the need to cling to her father. He no longer represented to her the sum of human affection. She saw him as a man who had perverted all his charming qualities — which were many — into a false dream of power. From his grasping authority she would surely escape.

She constantly found justification for her attitude. Her father, finding Browning with her one afternoon, though he said nothing direct either then or in the evening when he again saw Elizabeth, nevertheless by his manner conveyed his displeasure to her. Rather, she felt — since he *could* not suspect their relationship or their plans, ought he to be grateful to this great poet who gave of his time and effort to amuse the invalid. On the whole she was *glad* that he no longer came to her room to say goodnight; she would feel like a hypocrite if he did. Though she tried to be fair to him she could with the finest casuistry find excuses for her deceit; for so far she did not deceive herself, to believe that she was not, in effect, lying to him. She had to justify the means by the end.

For the end was a worthy one. It was not mere gratification of a fancied partiality or a sentimental attachment (like Henrietta's). By every test this was true love. And not only did it open for her the gates of life itself, promising to release her from her prison of invalidism, to take

her out into the world of people, of music and art — all
hitherto closed to her — but it offered her the opportunity
to make the most of this talent of hers which, however
weak it might really be, seemed of worth both to her
father and her lover. Her father would stifle it by keeping her shut up in London fog and damps; her lover
offered her the sensible way out — Italy. Had he not
written: "I look forward to a real life's work for us
both"? They would stimulate each other to ever greater
effort; if she could better her own poetry, if by her
influence she could make his great poetry greater, would
not the world be the richer? Even now he felt that she
helped him; his *Luria* and *Soul's Tragedy* already bore
her stamp.

So she argued herself into acquiescence borne along
on the tides of her own emotion and his passionate love.
In letters they could still discuss ideas, books, and people
though again and again they were sidetracked with perverse interpretations of each other's phrases or sentiments.
In their interviews, which now came twice a week whenever the danger of interruption by Mr. Barrett or the
somewhat suspicious Mr. Kenyon did not threaten, in
these hours they did "not even *talk* much now." After
all, as Browning quaintly remarked "you can't kiss
Mind!" All the talking could be done on paper. Their
moments together were too precious and too few to be
wasted with serious conversation.

At first they had both been divided between desire
and fear. Browning's Mildred and Mertoun in *A Blot
in the Scutcheon* could hurry toward a consummation

that in their youth and their inexperience they but half suspected. Wiser lovers hesitate, half fearful of what is to come. Light lovers rush into each other, seizing all at once; Browning and Elizabeth drank a slow deep draught.

And when, after a mild winter, spring came, their love flamed until Browning cried out: "Oh, dearest, let us marry soon, very soon, and end all this!" fearful of Elizabeth's tendency to magnify to the point of tears the slight differences which would occur between them. Could he see her every day he would drown her morbid fears in kisses. She never misunderstood him when he spoke; letters were prone to misinterpretation.

"But *do* think, my own Ba," he wrote, "any obstacle now, would be more than I could bear — I feel I *must* live with you, — if but for a year, a month — to express the love which words cannot express, nor these letters, nor aught else."

Such language could hardly be misunderstood; this lover was no mystic wooer satisfied to worship from afar. "I kneel to you, my Ba," he began decorously — "and pray you to give yourself to me in deed as in word — the body as the heart and mind, — and now!" This language set her blood tingling, her heart leaping. It was pleasant to find herself desired as other women were, but such desire was disquieting. Just now she was witnessing the emotions caused by a young girl's marriage. Hordes of relatives had descended upon Wimpole Street to attend the wedding of one of their clan. Though Elizabeth shrank from the excitement of the performance, though she somewhat scorned all the fuss and flurry, she was deeply interested in the conversation and the emotional reactions of aunts and uncles. The bride's mother was in tears. Marriage — for women — obviously held something of terror. All the gaiety was but the shadow hiding the truth. And Elizabeth was forty, no young girl to enter lightly upon who knows what depths of intimacy.

Sometimes Browning would urge her to marry him at once "merely as to form" that he might claim her if need arose, that he might claim the privilege of being beside her in case of illness, that he might interpose should her father prove more than usually tyrannical ! "Merely as to form"; that was a way out. But, alas, it would not do. Browning could not have his rights recognized by her father unless he revealed the marriage; and at that very moment of confession he would be saved the trouble of coming upstairs to her room by having her thrown bodily out of the window to him; and then he would be welcome to pick up the pieces, put them in a bag, and trot off to Nova Zembla with them.

No, this would not do. She would marry him — in time — but perhaps this year she had best go to Italy with Mrs. Jameson, that kind-hearted literary lady who was friendly with them both and who repeatedly had desired to be of service as courier to the invalid poetess. This was not to Browning's liking; he claimed her promise. Well, then, would it not be wisdom to ask Mrs. Jameson to accompany them ? to share with him the burden of her weakness ? Here Elizabeth knew that she was playing for time, time to get used to the idea of marriage. To his passionate plea, "Oh let us be alone, Ba," she yielded. Surely he would be a gentle lover then as now. She would have some little privacy left — he himself desired a separate dressing-room for he had so written: "I could never brush my hair and wash my face, I do think, before my own father — I could not, I am sure, take off my coat before you *now* — why should I ever ?"

Perhaps after all she exaggerated her fears. Yet she could not be immediately decisive. The force of his love frightened her; her self-distrust made her feel that if she took him at his word and married him at once he might repent. Nevertheless, though she fenced for time, she redoubled her efforts to gain strength, trying her physical powers by walking up and down stairs almost every day. She went shopping and bought a hat (which meant more goings out to wear it); and finally she drove to the park to walk upon the grass. These efforts were definitely preparation for the flight abroad. From time to time her heart misgave her. She would never be strong enough, she would never have the necessary resolution. She had need of Browning's constant encouragement especially when her father would show her kindnesses, would bring her flowers which, being neglected, would fade long before Browning's roses.

Life at home was clearly becoming impossibly complicated. If she were to keep this new-gained health she must get away from these fears and frights; Mr. Kenyon with his lately acquired spectacles was altogether too inquisitive; he would advise her to instruct the servants when they refused callers admittance not to give as their reason that Mr. Browning was with Miss Barrett. Besides, the open season for sentimentalists was on. She was constantly visited by lesser literary lights or would-be poetesses and authors or feminine hero-worshippers who would come and stay, in spite of her evident weariness, two and three hours, sometimes chatting fast and furiously, sometimes sitting and staring, and finally departing after protests of undying regard and unwelcome kisses. There were hosts of letters, too, from sensible admirers and senseless adorers, some among them silly men who on the strength of her reputation as a poet would offer heart and hand and promise eternal love as they might a dish of sweetmeats. Elizabeth had sufficient human sympathy not to disregard even the most foolish of her pseudo admirers. She would patiently answer letters, would kindly criticize the manuscripts sent her, would let herself be teased into consent for interviews. "If we mayn't come in," pleaded the more insistent, "will you stand up at the window that we may see?" Once this adulation might have pleased her faintly; at least it amused her. Now she found it tiring and annoying.

More annoying still were the rumors brought into the house by her brothers from their excursions into social London that Browning had some years previously been engaged, was now engaged to a different person, was, indeed, to be immediately married to this second love, a certain Miss Campbell. This idle tale she was not allowed to overlook. On Sunday when as usual all the Barrett brood invaded Elizabeth's room for half an hour (during the week they came by twos and threes) Alfred with assumed solemnity asked her what she knew about it, and at her somewhat indignant denial, threw himself upon a sofa declaring that he would now become ill himself so that some delightful young lady would seek him out and pay him court. Elizabeth was too sensible to be troubled by idle rumors in the face of Browning's devotion to her; yet they caused a faint ripple of fear. He and she could not shut themselves away from the world. The time was fast coming when she must exert herself. They were not skilful enough in their lying, he who abhorred all deception, and she who had from infancy been trained in it; it was becoming more and more difficult to manage Mr. Kenyon. Browning was all for throwing themselves on his mercy. Elizabeth felt that Kenyon would then entreat her not to ruin Browning's career by burdening him with an invalid for wife. He might suspect their intimacy; he could not, she felt sure, suspect their actual engagement.

So the long summer dragged on. To no one did Elizabeth speak the full truth (even her sisters could not know quite all for fear of their father's wrath) except her old blind friend, Mr. Boyd. Now that she was daily driving out into the world, going to see the flowers in the park, to wonder at the railroad, walking to post her own letters to Browning, she took to visiting Boyd as of old. With the intuition of sightless people he questioned her: was she going into a nunnery? or was she planning to get married ? Sure of his secrecy — besides he had few visitors who knew her — she confided in him. Not only did he bind himself to silence but he bound her to a promise that she would not alter her purpose, that she would in very truth embark upon this great adventure. Though she knew he was interested chiefly in having her break the chain of parental authority, still she derived comfort from his approval.

One other old friend had begun to suspect. This was "Treppy," little old Miss Trepsack who dined with the Barretts every Sunday as well as many a time during the week, scolding them all impartially and permitting them to coax her back into good humor. Treppy was a Creole who had lived, an adopted favorite, in the house of Mr. Barrett's grandfather in Jamaica. That grandfather she pictured to the Barrett children as a true hero in the days when men were giants. With an income of fifty thousand pounds a year he had on principle worn clothes patched on knee and elbow. His father had been an even more magnificent man, one who had "flogged his slaves like a divinity; and upon the beatitude of slaves as slaves, let no one presume to doubt, before Treppy. If ever she sighs over the slaves, it is to think of their emancipation. Poor creatures, to be emancipated !"

Treppy had been the closest friend of Mr. Barrett's mother; before her he could not pose as a tyrant. And of all his brood none was so dear to her as Elizabeth. This summer of Elizabeth's hesitancy Treppy was particularly difficult. She was constantly asserting that no one cared for her any more; she was old and deaf and unnecessary to the Barretts' happiness. It took all gentle Arabel's patience to reassure her that the whole family really loved and revered her and could not get along without her. She was mollified. But they needn't think they were pulling any wool over *her* eyes. She smelt marriage. Elizabeth and Henrietta were going to be sensible at last.

But Elizabeth could hardly dash off like the heroines of the romances she devoured. Such damsels had only to spring upon their lovers' horses and gallop off into the future. In some forest glade they would find perfect happiness, unmindful of the morrow. No need had they for clothes or toothbrushes or bankers' checks; no need to leave a forwarding address with the postman. They loved; their love was opposed; they leapt into lovers' arms and were off. Elizabeth's problem was less simple. She and her lover must lay their plans craftily to escape detection, and they must make prudent provision for their food and shelter. To Italy they would go, but not as mad young people who fall into difficulties and have to send post-haste for parental forgiveness and funds. To Italy they would go; but they would take Flush, and Wilson, Elizabeth's maid, and the necessary personal belongings — and surely their dearest loved books.

Elizabeth made cautious inquiries of her brothers to find out exactly what her fortune was. She had been spending what seemed to her a fairly extravagant amount, the largest being Wilson's eighteen pounds a year, and a heavy expenditure for morphine. Clothes, even when she was well enough to go out, had never been of great interest or expense; she liked quiet elegance, but one grand gown lasted long. Five-shilling dresses satisfied her fully. Presumably Flush would not continue to be stolen and cost six guineas' redemption !

She found that she had ordinarily received but a fraction of her income, while her capital had steadily been increased. Eight thousand pounds of her money was invested in the Funds at low interest; besides this there was an income of two hundred pounds a year ship money, hitherto untouched; recently Mr. Barrett had decided to invest this income for her in the new railroad which paid a fabulous rate of interest. Although he controlled her fortune, doling out to her only the smaller part of her income, Mr. Barrett scrupulously registered everything in her name, so that there would be no real difficulty in gaining command of her resources. Only she dared not ask while she was under her father's roof; and as she had imprudently used up last quarter's income she would have nothing until October. Obviously she could not depart with Browning until then, as after all they must have funds.

This difficulty was immediately surmounted. The Brownings, though far from possessing wealth like Mr. Barrett's, and though naturally uncertain of the wisdom of marriage with an invalid, were happy to help their son, being wholly in his confidence. Browning's father placed at his disposal more than enough money for the journey to Italy. At this time Browning had no fixed income; his receipts from poetry were negligible and other occupation he had none. He had thought that, to support a wife, he had best apply for a diplomatic post.

This suggestion was straightway vetoed by Elizabeth. How could she be happy if she were the means of tying him down to an office desk instead of leaving him free to devote himself to poetry ?   Besides, the idea was absurdly unnecessary. There would be no mine and thine with them. Her income would be ample for them both in Italy. Confident that with Elizabeth always with him his productiveness would be increased to provide an income from his poems (had not Moxon said that they were at last selling ?) Browning agreed to seek no employment.

Sensitive, however, lest the world and Mr. Barrett should criticize him unfavorably for having profitted financially by his marriage, Browning asked her to protect his pride by willing her property to her sisters. He had at first asked her to transfer it to them at once, and rely on his earning powers; he was not obstinate enough to insist upon this when she pointed out that if she renounced her income she might become a burden to him, especially if she were ill; and in any case the necessity for remunerative work would impair his poetical productivity. If he insisted, she would will everything to her sisters, after his death. To this he urged that if he were unlucky enough to survive her he would not want her money; he would need to be poor that he might lose himself in hard work. Elizabeth, however, was firm. After his death the money might revert to her family, not before.

She wrote and signed her document, sending it to Browning, who folded it away, but not without one last teasing word: "There may be even a *claimant,* instead of a recipient, of whatever either of us can bequeath — who knows ?"

Elizabeth's inquiries had started up her brothers' curiosity. Was she really going to try an Italian trip in spite of her father's veto ? Who would go with her ? Fearful of their suspecting the truth Elizabeth thought it necessary to reduce the frequency of Browning's visits; she tried to be satisfied with one a week, and failed. Browning made a thorough investigation of boats and trains; they discussed the advantages of sea and land travel. Finally they decided upon crossing to Paris whence they could proceed to Pisa as seemed best at the time. Browning grew impatient; they were risking so much to see each other once or twice a week; would it not be better to take the whole risk quickly and gain all ?

Elizabeth still hung fire. She prepared her mind for the marriage by attending services at the chapel. She was sure that she would never have the strength for marriage and flight on the same day. She would marry him, and then as soon as she had regained something of composure, she would go to Italy with him. She would want to get out of England at once, as far as possible from gossiping tongues and an insanely angry father; but she would need a little time to pull her nerves together. During that interval she would not see him; she would be too fearful of discovery. If her father knew, he might part them even then; she must be far away when his wrath thundered.

In the end it was she who proposed immediate marriage. For years the Wimpole Street house had been in sad need of extensive repairs; Mr. Barrett had frequently talked of sending the family away for a period of house-cleaning and painting. Now, in September, whether because he had become suspicious of Elizabeth and Henrietta, or because the state of the house finally seemed to him unbearable (although Elizabeth thought it little worse than a year or two before), he sent one of his sons off to Reigate to hire a house there or anywhere else he thought pleasant, anywhere to remove the family from London. His one month would easily turn into two or six or twelve, they all knew. Once he had got them away he would not permit their return until the London house had been turned upside down and remade entirely to his satisfaction.

Elizabeth was frightened. Though she was no longer positively ill, she was still delicate; she was weak and nervous with scant ability to endure fatigue. She dared not attempt a journey to Italy later than October or November. This coming winter would hardly duplicate the mildness of that of the preceding year; it might in its severity deprive her of her new-found strength and throw her back into the old lassitude; it would take a summer to repair its damages on her health. There would be a whole year gone, a year which she might have had in Italy with the man she loved utterly.

All this she hinted in her troubled letter of Wednesday night ending, "It seems quite too soon and too sudden for us to set out on our Italian adventure now — and perhaps even we could not compass —

"Well — but you must think for both of us. It is past twelve and I have just a moment to seal this and entrust it to Henrietta for the morning's post."

A postscript really settled the matter: "I will do as you wish — understand."

In two days and a half Elizabeth Barrett was Mrs. Robert Browning. With Wilson she had driven to Marylebone Church on Saturday morning, half fainting with excitement. Thrilled over the romance, Wilson stopped at the chemist's on the way to administer sal volatile to her trembling mistress. At quarter of eleven on the 12th of September, 1846, Elizabeth met Browning for the ninety-first time, the last time that they ever met to part.

Elizabeth took refuge at Mr. Boyd's house, mercifully finding him occupied so that she had time to rest before the need of talking. The elated Wilson was sent home to ask Henrietta and Arabel to call for their sister. That her sisters might afterwards truthfully say that they did not know of her marriage Elizabeth had forborne to confide in them. So now she could not let them see her agitation; she must quiet her nerves and pretend to be calm. By the time her sisters, somewhat puzzled and perturbed over Elizabeth's unexplained absence, arrived, Elizabeth, fortified by Cyprus wine and the calm conversation of Mr. Boyd, could meet their searching inquiries and could nerve herself to accompany them on a drive.

The next morning all her brothers piled into her room for their usual Sunday visit. With them came two or three old friends. Because she had so much to conceal Elizabeth did not dare plead indisposition to avoid their

company or even to quiet their frightful din. Marylebone Church bells rang the hour before they left her.
She had done no more than commence a letter to her
husband when Mr. Kenyon, spectacles on nose, came in,
beginning the conversation by an abrupt query: "When
did you see Browning?" Skilled in the use of half-truths
Elizabeth answered quietly: "He was here on Friday,"
and swiftly changed subject. Before he went away Mr.
Kenyon returned to the charge: "When do you see
Browning again?" Elizabeth could answer somewhat
gleefully and wholly truthfully: "I do not know," for
her seeing him depended upon his plans for their Italian
journey.

Both Browning and his wife were confused these days
when, though married, they were completely separated,
communicating only by letter. Neither could think
clearly, working under the greatest excitement because of
emotional strain and the need of secrecy. Browning
mixed up days and hours and railroads with magnificent
disregard for anything but their swift escape. Elizabeth
with Wilson's help packed and plotted, aided by the de-
lay in the Barrett plans for removal. Somehow Wilson
managed to get out of the house and into Browning's
hands such luggage as she and her mistress considered
indispensable. Somehow for all his confusion Browning
managed to find a schedule of trains that would permit
Elizabeth to leave her father's house at a time when her
going would not be immediately noticed. On Saturday,
the 20th of September, during the dinner hour of the
Barretts, while she was supposedly dining in her room,

Elizabeth crept downstairs, fearful lest Flush make a noise, gained the street unseen, hailed a cab, and was off to meet her husband from whom she was never again in life to be separated.

In her last letter to Browning, written the night before, Elizabeth had said: "By to-morrow at this time, I shall have *you* only, to love me — my beloved!

"You *only!* As if one said *God only.*"

CHAPTER VII

IN THE week between marriage and flight, Elizabeth had had time to think through her problem. Having refused to let Browning see her, she experienced life without hope of his coming; she knew now that without him life was unbearable; that all the affection of her brothers and sisters, even the full love of her father were it to be restored to her, would no longer suffice. And so when she shut the door of Wimpole Street behind her, it was not with regret for what she was losing, but with joy for what she was gaining. As that night she watched the shores of England recede there was room in her heart for nothing beyond her intense love for Robert Browning.

Before she had reached Paris her father would have found her letter to him, that letter in which she had dared ask his forgiveness — which eventually he must grant. And all London would soon know, since Browning had prepared the proper advertisement (dateless save for "Saturday" that it might seem to have been the day of their departure) and had ordered made and sent to all friends the proper announcements. They had taken every precaution to spare themselves and Mr. Barrett the embarrassment of having it known that they had been married a week before leaving for France and Italy. This marriage of theirs must not be labelled elopement, nor must it be the subject for gossip.

Gossip there necessarily was when two prominent poets married without warning. "So," said Wordsworth, "Elizabeth Barrett and Robert Browning have gone off together. Well, I hope they understand each other." Mr. Horne now knew why Elizabeth had recently refused to see him, even after he had threatened to bring his guitar and play to her sisters if she continued obdurate. Little Miss Mitford had new food for thought and chatter. Mr. Kenyon whom both Browning and Elizabeth had feared, feeling that he would consider it his duty to keep them apart for both their sakes, cheered them by an immediate note applauding their resolution. He said that Elizabeth had risked her life, but that she had done well in so risking it.

In Wimpole Street only Arabel and Henrietta remained sympathetic. Mr. Barrett, observing bitterly that it would better have become Elizabeth to prepare for the next world, dismissed her from his heart forever. He never saw her again; the letters which she wrote him from time to time were returned unopened. To show his family and the world his unconcern Mr. Barrett adopted the gaiest of manners and began a series of dinner parties. Elizabeth could forgive his silence, having been prepared for it. What was hard to understand was the resentment of her brothers, especially of George who had himself impressed upon her her father's indifference, when the Italian journey of last winter had been forbidden.

There were, however, no further shadows on her happiness. At last there was no need to spring up startled when the door opened; no need to dissemble, to count the days till Tuesday, to pack all the loving into three scant hours. How cleverly they had dissembled they saw in the astonishment of Mrs. Jameson whose friendly offers as courier to Italy Elizabeth had declined only a week before. Mrs. Jameson was herself an assiduous writer; she had long since endeared herself to Browning by her praise of Elizabeth into whose privacy she had won entry by sheer persistence. Elizabeth, at first prejudiced against her as one more incense-burner, had eventually come to return her liking. Mrs. Jameson now smoothed for the poets their path to Pisa.

From Pisa Elizabeth wrote to Miss Mitford: "I have been neither much wiser nor much foolisher than all the shes in the world, only much happier — the difference is in the happiness."

And happiness it was. Browning was ever at her side; though she was well enough to walk, he carried her upstairs for pure pleasure of his burden. The days and weeks went by as in a dream. The journey to Pisa with new scenes spread before her had been tiring as well as exciting; once there life became a simple matter of enjoyment. Her whole duty, as Browning seemed to define it, was to let herself be carried upstairs, to sit on a sofa, and not to step in a puddle when they were out walking. Browning was bent upon spoiling her as he had already spoiled Flush who, no longer suspicious as in Wimpole Street, had no need of Elizabeth's scoldings and Wilson's slaps to teach him not to bite Browning. Flush took to liberty kindly, running joyously through the streets, fraternizing with Italian dogs, bringing home whole hordes of fleas which, to relieve his torture, Browning and Elizabeth, sitting on the floor with a basin of water, patiently combed out. And when his philanderings and the unaccustomed heat of Italy deprived Flush of his long silky hair and with it his beauty, neither he nor his mistress grieved.

Once in England, she had almost lost her wits when Flush had been stolen and had not been returned by the dog-stealer according to promise. She had rushed downstairs and had with difficulty been dissuaded from trying to run to the thief's house in the fast-coming dark. And when her brother who went in her place came back without Flush, she had been hysterical; and had next day gone in a cab with no one but Wilson, to demand her pet. Now she let Flush trot about without fear; London dog-stealers could not catch him here; and if he stayed away overnight, why, he would return. So soon had she lost her extra set of nerves and come to look at the world more calmly.

She even learned, when Wilson caught a fever, that she could comb her own hair, lace her own stays, and hook up her own dress; even make toast and water for the invalid though Browning carried the kettle for her and instructed her how to toast bread without setting fire to it.

Housekeeping cares had she none. Browning saw to the ordering of fires in their rooms morning and night; he arranged for their dinner which consisted poetically of thrushes and chianti, sent in at two o'clock from a neighboring restaurant. At six came coffee and rolls made of milk; at nine they supped on roast chestnuts and grapes. Eggs could always be relied on for breakfast; and there they were — "the prophet Elijah or the lilies of the field took as little thought for their dining."

They lived in a perpetual tête-à-tête and did not weary of each other. For these two had more than love to bind them; they had a community of interests. With their common literary tastes, their similar minds (they whom the critics found obscure were never cryptic to each other), they were friends and companions as well as lovers.

And now at Pisa Browning at last learned that the time of their courting had not, as he had feared, been poetically barren for Elizabeth. Again and again he had questioned her about her writing, being always told to wait. He had offered his shoulder as writing desk: "I wish, dearest," he had written in the summer before their marriage, "you would tell me precisely what you have written — all my affectionate pride in you rises at once when I think of your poetry, that is and that is to be — you dear, dear Ba, can you not write on my shoulder while my head lies as you permit ?"

Her strong sense of delicacy and reserve had prevented her showing him what she was writing on her microscopic slips of paper. One morning at Pisa she tucked into his coat pocket a packet of forty-four of these slips, on each written in her tiny script a love sonnet. She was gone when he began to read.

The opening sonnet at once struck the note that recurred constantly, the conquering of Death by Love:

> I thought how Theocritus had sung
> Of the sweet years, the dear and wished-for years,
> Who each one in a gracious hand appears
> To bear a gift for mortals, old or young:
> And, as I mused it in his antique tongue,
> I saw, in gradual vision through my tears,
> The sweet, sad years, the melancholy years,
> Those of my own life, who by turns had flung
> A shadow across me. Straightway I was 'ware,
> So weeping, how a mystic Shape did move
> Behind me, and drew me backward by the hair,
> And a voice said in mastery while I strove, . . .
> "Guess now who holds thee ? " — "Death," I said. But, there
> The silver answer rang. . . "Not Death, but Love."

This was not mere rhetoric. For years Elizabeth had been accustomed to think of herself as one on the very brink of the grave; her friends, her family, even her doctors had considered her too frail for any length of normal life. It was, therefore, only natural that she should sing in these poems of the differences between herself, pallid dweller in half-ruined house, and this princely lover whose destiny led him out into the world which he would conquer; only Death could level their lots. In the very ashes of grief she sat; farther off he ought to go, lest he be scorched by their dying fire. She could not forbear adding that though he would, of course, go, she would always feel him near; even in God's presence at last she would plead for him in one breath with herself.

Having thus by the end of the sixth sonnet shown

the impossibility of their fitting union Elizabeth proceeded to show how the "face of all the world" had been changed by love. What could she give her lover in return for the gold and purple of his heart? The colors of her life had become pale and dead from tears, not fitting stuff for a pillow for his head; he had far better trample upon it. "Can it be right to give what I can give?" she queried. "I will not soil thy purple with my dust." And yet she loved.

Love is beautiful, the sonnets continue. Only in her love is she worthy, worthy to renounce him. Indeed even her love is not her own; she learned it from him. That love she could not voice:

> Nay, let the silence of my womanhood
> Commend my woman-love to thy belief.

And then comes the plea of love for love's sake, the old longing of her girlhood to be loved "just because":

> If thou must love me, let it be for nought
> Except for love's sake only. Do not say
> "I love her for her smile . . . her look . . . her way
> Of speaking gently, . . . for a trick of thought
> That falls in well with mine, and certes brought
> A sense of pleasant ease on such a day" —
> For these things in themselves, Belovèd, may
> Be changed, or change for thee, — and love, so wrought,
> May be unwrought so. Neither love me for
> Thine own dear pity's wiping my cheeks dry, —
> A creature might forget to weep, who bore
> Thy comfort long, and lose thy love thereby!
> But love me for love's sake, that evermore
> Thou mayst love on, through love's eternity.

ROBERT AND ELIZABETH BROWNING

From the colored crayons by Lowes Dickinson

Again the sonnets emphasize the difference between his freedom, her imprisonment; he could be sure of her love, dared she be sure of his ? At his bidding she will cease to strive, hoping that his love will enlarge her worth. And yet perhaps she ought to be to him

> A hope, to sing by gladly? . . . or a fine
> Sad memory, with thy songs to interfuse?
> A shade, in which to sing . . . of palm or pine ?
> A grave, on which to rest from singing ? . . . Choose.

Two sonnets follow which one could wish had been still-born. Elizabeth voices maidenly reluctance to part with a lock of her hair and maidenly romantic rejoicing over the acceptance of a lock of her lover's hair which, cherished henceforth in her bosom, will never lack natural heat until her death. Hers he is to take

> . . . finding pure, from all those years,
> The kiss my mother left here when she died.

Fortunately the sonnets quickly regain lost dignity and power:

> Say thou love me, love me, love me — toll
> The silver iterance ! only minding, dear,
> To love me also in silence, with thy soul.

Heaven would be less perfect than love on this imperfect earth; since her lover would grieve to lose her:

> I yield the grave for thy sake, and exchange
> My near sweet view of Heaven, for earth with thee !

So great is their love that it will endure forever:

> God only, who made us rich, can make us poor.

Once more the thought of death creeps in; she had lived among visions; there was no future for her but death until love, strong as death, came to make her safe and strong and glad. She has twined about her lover as a vine about a tree; weeping she wonders if she but dreams his love. In his presence all fears dissolve, even those which doubted the enduring quality of his love. Her pet name causes another lapse in the tone of the sonnets, which rise once more with

> If I leave all for thee, wilt thou exchange
> And be all to me ? Shall I never miss
> Home-talk and blessing and the common kiss
> That comes to each in turn, nor count it strange,
> When I look up, to drop on a new range
> Of walls and floors . . . another home than this ?
> Nay, wilt thou fill that place by me which is
> Filled by dead eyes too tender to know change ?
> That's hardest. If to conquer love, has tried
> To conquer grief, tries more . . . as all things prove;
> For grief indeed is love and grief beside.
> Alas, I have grieved so I am hard to love.
> Yet love me — wilt thou ? Open thine heart wide,
> And fold within, the wet wings of my dove.

With even surer touch she pleads that her love may not harm him. Her doubts he conquered with the first kiss; her gratitude grows ever greater. He has given her such love as she had not believed existed; love as she had seen it in the world was a little thing. Once more comes the thought of her changed life; she had been ready for death and now writes new her "future's epigraph." She recounts the many ways she loves him, and concludes:

Belovèd, thou hast brought me many flowers
Plucked in the garden, all the summer through
And winter, and it seemed as if they grew
In this close room, nor missed the sun and showers.
So, in the like name of that love of ours,
Take back these thoughts which here unfolded too,
And which on warm and cold days I withdrew
From my heart's ground.   Indeed, those beds and bowers
Be overgrown with bitter weeds and rue,
And wait thy weeding; yet here's eglantine,
Here's ivy ! — take them, as I used to do
Thy flowers, and keep them where they shall not pine.
Instruct thine eyes to keep their colors true,
And tell thy soul, their roots are left in mine.

His first wonder let Browning accept these sonnets for what they were, intimate outpourings of a full heart, meant for his eye alone.   Elizabeth had never been one to share her emotions with the world; she was an intellectual, not a lyric, poet.   As her husband read again and yet again he was the more impressed with the universality of these poems in which she had without restraint expressed her innermost self.   Proud as he was to have a secret record of her devotion, he yet felt that he had no right to such a hoard.   This was true treasure; it ought not to lie hidden from the world.

At first when he suggested publication Elizabeth was adamant.   These poems were as truly his, as truly secret, as the letters she had written him.   She could and did share with the world her intellectual ideas; she could write for the world a fictitious love story; her emotions and her own love story were not public property.   He did not consider it necessary to justify her long hours of letter-writing by publication; why could he not feel as she did that these were merely letters to him ? These were different, he urged; they were the finest sonnets since Shakespeare ! She smiled. He urged and reurged their unparallelled literary value. She was not convinced. He over-valued them as he over-valued her. He was prejudiced by his feelings for her. Besides, they were not suitable for publication; they were her whisperings to him.

Had they been written originally for publication she could not thus have shown her heart. She was not one whose feelings, bubbling lightly up, could froth and sparkle for a delighted public. Her emotions were personal, not of the stuff of which public poems are made. To publish his heart's deepest outpourings the poet must, unless he be insincere, divorce the idea of himself from the emotion; he must universalize his emotional experience. Elizabeth wrote these sonnets as the outlet for her emotional crisis. It is because the experience, though rare in such perfect form, is the universal ideal that her poems remain the perpetual voice of true lovers. It was her husband who, in later years, expressed this reluctance to make copy of oneself:

Shall I sonnet-sing you about myself ?
  Do I live in a house you would like to see ?
Is it scant of gear, has it store of pelf ?
  "Unlock my heart with a sonnet-key ? "

Invite the world, as my betters have done ?
  "Take notice: this building remains on view,
Its suites of reception every one,
  Its private apartment and bedroom too;

"For a ticket, apply to the Publisher."
　　No: thanking the public, I must decline.
A peep through my window, if folk prefer;
　　But, please you, no foot over threshold of mine!

I have mixed with a crowd and heard free talk
　　In a foreign land where an earthquake chanced
And a house stood gaping, naught to balk
　　Man's eye wherever he gazed or glanced.

The whole of the frontage shaven sheer,
　　The inside gaped: exposed to day,
Right and wrong and common and queer,
　　Bare, as the palm of your hand, it lay.

The owner? Oh, he had been crushed, no doubt!
　　"Odd tables and chairs for a man of wealth!
What a parcel of musty old books about!
　　He smoked,—no wonder he lost his health!

"I doubt if he bathed before he dressed.
　　A brasier?—the pagan, he burned perfumes!
You see it is proved, what the neighbours guessed
　　His wife and himself had separate rooms."

Friends, the goodman of the house at least
　　Kept house to himself till an earthquake came:
'Tis the fall of its frontage permits you feast
　　On the inside arrangement you praise or blame.

Outside should suffice for evidence:
　　And whoso desires to penetrate
Deeper, must dive by the spirit-sense—
　　No optics like yours, at any rate!

"Hoity-toity! A street to explore,
　　Your house the exception? *'With this same key
Shakespeare unlocked his heart,'* once more!"
　　Did Shakespeare? If so, the less Shakespeare he!

So might Elizabeth have said, she who did not readily express her inner self in verse. In prose, in intimate letters, she could write herself out. In poetry, which was her medium of expression to the world at large, she insisted upon being impersonal. The *Sonnets from the Portuguese* were her one attempt to express poetically the intimate emotions of the moment. The *De Profundis* which beautifully records her grief over the death of her favorite brother was not written till the wound was partly healed and the emotion "recollected in tranquillity."

Her political poems did, indeed, record immediate emotion, but wrath and joy over revolutions and politicians are, however keen, not of the same intimacy as personal affections. She could later, without embarrassment, publish *Casa Guidi Windows,* recording in it her first impressions of and reactions to Italian politics in 1848 and her somewhat changed impressions three years later. Italy and freedom were both passions; but political passion was quite another matter from personal love and grief.

These sonnets were the most intimate writing she had ever done, with the exception of her letters to Browning. Decidedly they were not to be published.

Browning obstinately returned to the charge. Ink faded; in time there would be no replacing them; he would learn them by heart but even so they would die with him. Where was her devotion to poetry that she could refuse to make it this singular contribution? So earnest was he, so persistent, that in the end she yielded, to give him pleasure. She consented to a very small private edition provided that the personal application be camouflaged by a pretence of translation. In that way she could be protected from the charge of immodesty. *Sonnets from the Bosnian* would do. No one knew Bosnian literature! Browning offered a better suggestion: *Sonnets from the Portuguese*. He chose this because of his fondness for her already published poem *Caterina to Camoens,* a love poem that moved him deeply. Camoens was a famous Portuguese poet; Caterina was to him what Elizabeth was to Browning.

Life continued to run smoothly for the poets who prudently lived within their income and managed to get through the days and weeks without fixed occupation and without boredom. There were sights for the once cloistered Elizabeth to see; there were new friends to meet, there were journeys to take, there were new poems to write. In the spring they went to Florence where all the English and Americans gathered; and then they sought the hills for coolness, plunging into the mountains to stay, they thought, two or three months at the monastery of Vallombrosa. The magnificence of the scenery did much in their poets' eyes to atone for the bread made apparently from the sawdust of the fir trees; bread that had a fetid odor which made them relinquish it for the beef and oil and wine which, though excellent, were hardly balanced diet. They had dreamt of eggs and bread and milk as suitable summer food; but "the hens had 'got them to a nunnery,' and objected to lay eggs, and the milk and the holy water stood confounded." Nevertheless, though the bread "stuck in the throat like Macbeth's amen" they would have stayed, feasting on mountains. The new abbot did not, however, sanction their desires. Three days were visitors allowed and not all Browning's eloquence could much extend them. After five days they were thrust out ignominiously. Elizabeth and her maid, being women, stank in the abbot's nostrils. He and his friars following the instructions of San Gualberto, founder of their order, might "attain to sanctification, among other means, by cleaning out pigsties with their bare hands, without spade or shovel; but *that* is uncleanliness enough — they wouldn't touch the little finger of a woman."

Driven out of Eden, wrote Elizabeth gaily; for had not Milton taken his description of Paradise from Vallombrosa? "To Florence, though! and what Florence is, the tongue of man or poet may easily fail to describe. The most beautiful of cities, with the golden Arno shot through the breast of her like an arrow, and 'non dolet' all the same. For what helps to charm here is the innocent gaiety of the people, who, for ever at feast day and holiday celebrations, come and go along the streets, the women in elegant dresses and with glittering fans, shining away every thought of Northern cares and taxes, such as make people grave in England. No little orphan on a house step but seems to inherit naturally his slice of watermelon and bunch of purple grapes, and the rich fraternize with the poor as we are unaccustomed to see them, listening to the same music and walking in the same gardens, and looking at the same Raphaels even!"

Here, settled in cool rooms in the Palazzo Guidi, they celebrated their first wedding anniversary. Elizabeth joyously excited over the Pope, the Grand Duke, and the new Tuscan freedom.

It was fitting that this new home of her adoption should ring with freedom. It was symbolic; here was she, a housebound invalid, suddenly released into a world of sunshine. Italy became an extension of herself, her new self strong in the strength of Browning's love.

For marriage had brought her no pain, no disillusionment. Fifteen months had passed since she left all the world she had ever known to seek new lands with this man she had known less than two years. She marvelled at her temerity, she who had ever been irresolute. She had thought she understood love; her father, she had once thought, loved her; Edward had certainly loved her. Yet Edward had turned his heart toward another woman; he had not found complete satisfaction in her as she had in him. Her father had never really loved her at all; in so far as she had gratified his pride he had been pleased with her; he had not known the love which seeks the happiness of the loved one. This love of Browning's was wholly different; it was absorbing to him as to her. They never wearied of each other though they were scarcely apart an hour in the day. What plans they made! They were idle now, both of them, having such great need of each other. There was so much to say, so much to leave unsaid. It was pleasant for her to lie still listening to his tocattas and fugues. Then they would take long drives, with Flush riding proudly past the little Italian dogs.

Gradually wonderment gave way to deep content. She no longer feared that this was a golden dream from which she would wake in Wimpole Street; it was incredible, but it was true. Her prince charming had waked her with a kiss, had caught her up upon his fairy horse, and had taken her into his kingdom. None of the heroines in the romantic novels she favored had ever fared more royally.

Fairy diet, however, failed to prove sufficient for a British husband; yet the coming of a man cook who served them mutton chops instead of thrushes caused her neither grief nor trouble; and the furnishing of an apartment was pure amusement. Six rooms in the Palazzo Guidi they had found, three of them of true palace proportions opening on a terrace. Their windows faced the grey wall of the church of San Felice — a good omen. Antique furnishings were obviously needed; and these the two poets set out to find with two winters' modest royalties of their poems as capital. Fifty pounds bought them "rococo chairs, spring sofas, carved bookcases, satin from cardinals' beds." Elizabeth had claimed first "a spring sofa to loll upon, and a supply of rain water to wash in; and you should see what a picturesque oil jar they have given us for the latter purpose. It would just hold the captain of the forty thieves."

Browning concentrated on tables and chairs, Elizabeth on chests of drawers, regardless of the possession of goods to fill them. Both took pleasure in the acquisition of a bookcase from a convent, all "carved-wood angels, infants and serpents," upon whose shelves when their modest means permitted they would put a whole set of Balzac, if the angels, infants, and serpents could be persuaded not to revolt.

After their labors they sought rest and coolness in Fano and in Ancona, only to be fairly withered by heat, Elizabeth reduced to lying on a sofa clad only in "a petticoat and a white dressingwrapper," divested of gown, stays, and shoes. Unlike her father Browning permitted dishabille. After three weeks of vain wanderings they returned to Florence where Elizabeth sank peacefully in her "sybaritically soft" chair.

That fall Browning frightened her by a month's illness of fever and sore throat. Now it was she who was the strong one, the protector and caretaker. So little accustomed was she to the rôle that she did not dare run counter to her husband and summon a physician. She could only hold his burning hands and bring him water and sit unhappily waiting and hoping for relief. And relief came through an unexpected source. A literary Jesuit — Mr. Mahoney, Father Prout, — travelling in Italy called upon the Brownings. Finding Browning ill and Mrs. Browning deeply troubled he calmly took charge. He pointed out to Elizabeth that lack of food had increased her husband's weakness until the fever was having its own way. What he needed was something to start building up his strength; with strength he would fight the fever and all would be well. So with his own hand he mixed up eggs in good port wine and persuaded the invalid to drink, while the Italian manservant raised his hands crying out, "O Inglesi, Inglesi !" and Elizabeth herself was more than half afraid of this "eccentric prescription." To her joy, however, it was of benefit; Browning drank and was soothed into sleep; and as he slept she held her hand on his wrist and noted that the pulse grew steadier and slower. Father Prout remained in Florence overseeing his patient and jesting with Elizabeth, calling her a "bambina" to be so thoroughly frightened. As Browning recovered Father Prout gave up doctoring and took to talking; he was not a cultivated gentleman, but a kindly good-hearted man, and withal learned. He had travelled widely, met every one worth knowing, and was a gushing fountain of amusing anecdote and apt quotation. When he departed for Rome he left behind one more devoted friend in Elizabeth whom he had first comforted and then charmed.

Now came rumors that Florence would be sacked. The Brownings remained interested bystanders not at all eager to flee, though the Grand Duke sent his family to the safety of Siena and the walls were chalked up with "Morte a Fiorentini !" The Pope was a fugitive, the crowned heads were poised for flight, anarchy was supposedly abroad. The Brownings were unafraid.

Elizabeth was forced to revise her opinions more than once. Pope Pius the Ninth who a year since had been for her "this new wonderful Pope, who is a great man and doing greatly," was now a poor Pope deeply pitied, "a weak man with the noblest and most disinterested intentions." In another month he was an "obstinate idiot" though still considered good and tender-hearted. Some time later he was "the old serpent . . . wriggling his venom into the heart of all possibilities of free thought and action."

Politics, however, even with the excitement of revolutions and occupations, were not of such absorbing interest as Robert Wiedeman Barrett Browning, born in Florence on the 9th of March, 1849, three days after Elizabeth's forty-third birthday. Here was that claimant to her fortune at whom Browning had jestingly hinted.

Nothing in her life had prepared her for this experience. She had supposed herself too old for love; but love had come. Beyond she had not looked. When the possibility of a child became a certainty she shared only faintly her husband's obvious anxiety. She knew that she was rather past the age when women bore first babies; yet with the vaguest notion of life processes she thought Browning's solicitude somewhat exaggerated. Nevertheless, it proved his true devotion; he was not one to neglect her now that she lolled more than ever on her sofa, given over to dreams. The joy of love's fulfilment was sufficient for her. Browning watched uneasily the far-away look in her eyes, fervently hoping that all would yet be well.

When, finally, he was assured of the safety of his wife and the reality of his son his exuberant spirits knew no bounds. It was a gay family in Casa Guidi, though Flush, gleaming with renewed and flealess curls, fattened on great bunches of the purple grapes he loved, chose to be deeply offended at the new arrival. For days he sulked jealously; it took a fortnight's coaxing to bring him back to the family fold. At first accepting the baby as a necessary evil he ended by becoming his devoted slave.

But a deep sadness struck close upon the household's rejoicings. Browning's mother, to whom he was devoted with more than the usual filial affection and whom he had not seen since his marriage, died suddenly. Though his sister Sarianna tempered the blow by writing of illness when death had already occurred, and of death only when she thought his mind prepared, Browning was completely prostrated. When he had been at home he had never failed to go to his mother's room to say good-night no matter how late the hour; he had looked forward to the time when he should take to her his perfect wife.

Elizabeth and his mother had never met. When during the months of their engagement he had queried the possibility of his mother's and sister's calling upon her at Wimpole Street she had demurred. She did not receive many people beyond relatives and oldtime neighbors such as were friends of the family. A few literary people had indeed forced themselves upon her. But it was well known that she did not willingly receive outsiders. If, then, it were known that she had received Mrs. Browning and Sarianna there would be food for gossip both abroad and in her own home. Since it was of the utmost importance to her peace of mind and to her resolution in holding to her engagement to avoid gossip, it would be better for them not to come. So she reasoned with

Browning, and as always he acquiesced. But she knew that her real reason for not seeing them was her shyness, and her vague fear that they, finding her unworthy, would not approve of his love for her. So they had not come. Nor could they come to the wedding. Elizabeth, always hoping that in the end her father would forgive her, wanted the circumstances to be such as to give him the least possible offence. Also she wished to make it impossible for him to pour his wrath upon anyone except herself and her husband. If Browning's immediate family were at the church, then Mr. Barrett could regard their presence as an evidence of Elizabeth's preferring the Brownings to her own family; and he would further have accused them of underhand dealings, connivings to marry their son to his daughter. The fact that she had money and he none made the matter still more delicate. Afraid of intimidating her, fearful of her lack of resolution to see the marriage through, and anxious to please her in everything, Browning made no protest. His father and mother accepted his explanations and let him make his plans without question. So it was that Elizabeth had never seen her husband's people.

Now three weeks after her baby's birth she wrote affectionate letters of sympathy to Sarianna Browning, telling of Browning's great grief. It was, she thought, the greater because of his great joy in his newly born son and in his wife's safety. He had written to his mother sure of her pleasure in hearing of her grandson, and that letter had not reached her in time. When it had come she was unconscious, and the news which would have made her happy she could not hear. As Elizabeth watched her husband's inordinate grief — for months she never found him alone that he was not in tears — she felt bitterly her own responsibility in separating him from this dearly loved mother, in preventing him from being with her at the time of her death. These were her reproaches to herself; certainly her husband never uttered or even thought them. He was unable at first to find consolation; he could not reconcile himself to a world that did not hold his mother. Not even the baby could interest him. Later he took comfort in the child, going to see him bathed every morning, and many a time carrying him in his arms up and down the terrace.

With a newcomer who required a special servant, the household became embarrassingly expensive. Elizabeth's income, at first princely, was no longer adequate. And poetry had not yet brought either of the Brownings any appreciable sums. Kind Mr. Kenyon came to the rescue. At Elizabeth's marriage Mr. Barrett had immediately refused to attend to her investments. Mr. Kenyon had thoughtfully volunteered to act as her agent and had taken over from Mr. Barrett all Elizabeth's funds. He was therefore aware that her income was far short of the two thousand pounds a year her brothers, along with the rest of middle-class Londoners, thought necessary for marriage. Still, in spite of his own considerable wealth, he knew that it was possible for the Brownings to live well enough in Italy if not in England; and he did not interfere until the baby's birth. Then in pure friendship he settled upon them an income of a hundred pounds a year, which they accepted, knowing that their so doing gave him as much pleasure as their refusal would have pained him. At his death years later Mr. Kenyon bequeathed to them ten thousand pounds, enough to assure them comfort always, and not enough wealth to be a burden to poets who liked to live without ostentation.

The death of Browning's mother in the spring of 1849 made a change in their plans. They had thought to go to England at last, where Elizabeth's sisters eagerly awaited their transformed Ba and her robust baby. For the little Wiedeman, despite his mother's frailty, was a strong, healthy child, fat and physically advanced beyond other infants. It would have been a joy to exhibit him to relatives and friends who could not but be astonished at her possession of such a baby. Browning, however, could not bear to go to England where his mother no longer awaited him. He had no will to go anywhere and would have stayed on apathetically at Florence where certainly affairs were not apathetic. In less than two months there had been two revolutions, the first, expelling the Grand Duke, the second, seven weeks later, recalling him. Elizabeth wrote ". . . we have had two revolutions here at Florence, Grand Duke out, Grand Duke in. The bells in the church opposite rang for both. They first planted a tree of liberty close to our door, and then they pulled it down. The same tune, sung under the windows, did for 'Viva la republica !' and 'Viva Leopoldo !' The genuine popular feeling is certainly for the Grand Duke ('O, santissima madre di Dio !' said our nurse, clasping her hands, 'how the people do love him !'); only nobody would run

146 ELIZABETH BARRETT BROWNING

the risk of a pin's prick to save the ducal throne. If the Leghornese . . . had not refused to pay at certain Florentine cafés, we shouldn't have had revolution the second, and all this shooting in the street! Dr. Harding, who was coming to see me, had time to get behind a stable door, just before there was a fall against it of four shot corpses; and Robert barely managed to get home across the bridges."

The chief inconvenience the Brownings felt from revolution and counter-revolution was the dilatoriness of the bookseller in procuring them more Balzac. Apparently he despaired of both republic and Grand Duchy and thought that, if the world were coming to an end anyhow, these foreigners could get along without any more books than they already had. For her part Elizabeth declared herself "blasée about revolutions and invasions." The baby grew fat indiscriminately whether Florence were sacked or no, whether the Austrian army came or the Grand Duke went. "A revolution made by boys and *vivas,* and unmade by boys and *vivas*" even though blood was shed in the unmaking was too ignoble to call out her sympathy.

She was more deeply disturbed over her father's continued silence. Before the birth of her child, realizing both her small strength and the difficulties of a first child for a woman in the forties, she had written to members of the family what might, she knew, be last messages. Most of her brothers had by now forgiven her and had written her; from her father she had had no sign of relenting. Yet after the birth of this, his only grandchild, he might perhaps listen to her. She wrote again, and when after a week the letter had not been sent back she hoped that it had been read. Her hope was vain. Henrietta was wrong in fancying that this estrangement was of little moment to Elizabeth. Her affections were deeply rooted; moreover she admired dominant personalities. Had her father really loved her, she thought that she could never have brought herself to displease him. Indeed she might never have loved away from him since she would have emptied her heart of all its powers of love by directing them all toward him. But she still loved him, and her sisters who remained loyal to her, and her brothers even though they blamed her. For her best happiness she needed her family. Nevertheless, she was happier with Browning than she ever had been or could have been with them. She who had been a poor sick thing scarce a pleasure to herself or them in her best years, was now a normal woman, living a normal life in the world; and surrounded with such love as few could know or possess since there were none equal to Browning and few that measured half his stature.

And so with England impossible this summer she devoted herself to persuading Browning to leave Florence and to seek comfort from his sorrow in new scenes. It was not until she assured him that she and the baby were really suffering from Florentine heat that he consented to move to Bagni di Lucca in the valley of the Arno. Here among the mountains Browning learned to grieve less. Elizabeth, having gained strength from childbearing, found that she could take long forest walks and climb mountains with her husband. Since her illness at fifteen she had never possessed a quarter of the strength that was now hers. Perhaps some of it came from the fact that no longer was her health the first consideration of the household. Her husband had been ailing since the shock of his mother's death — he had lost sleep and appetite; and Elizabeth had exerted herself to coax him out of his melancholy, back into health. Then Wilson had defaulted and instead of hanging over her mistress, worried over the least sigh, had taken to bending over the cradle, self-appointed guardian of the baby. Even Flush had by now deserted, finding it highly diverting to be used as a pony. He would turn his head and gently kiss the little bare heels that kicked his glossy sides. Wiedeman was a merry child, friendly with all the world. At the age when most babies could not yet sit up he was trying to stand. He was king; Elizabeth was demoted to lady-in-waiting. This transference of attention diverted her mind from the state of her health. And indubitably she was stronger.

Yet she could not entirely renovate her physique after years of confinement, lack of exercise, and improper diet — in the old days at Wimpole Street many a time Flush had been called upon to eat a whole dinner of which his mistress would have none. And whereas in summer Elizabeth could walk and take long excursions up the side of mountains, seated uncertainly on a donkey, the winter of 1849 in Florence found her once more housebound. She had too long had the habit of dreading winds and fresh air to believe it possible that they were harmless. And so she remained indoors, not, however as of old, confined to bed or sofa.

She had not overcome her indolent habits, and loved to curl up in soft chair or loll on sofas, but she did move about. For occupation she had her poetry; and now she was preparing a new edition of her poems from volumes already published and from new material. And then, for the present more absorbing than poetry, there was little Wiedeman who, after a summer of mountaineering, had been brought back to Florence radiating health and good spirits; by the time he was six months old able to understand the English of his parents and the Italian of his voluble nurse who talked so much by day that Elizabeth was sure she must talk in her sleep, her tongue being quite unused to rest.

Sometimes Elizabeth's mirth found vent in Browning's sound scolding of such a careless wife. "Oh, Ba, I really can't trust you !" he exclaimed throwing down his newspaper to catch and comfort the baby who had rolled over on the floor, hitting his head. Elizabeth herself was not above teasing this adored infant of hers when she found that he grew jealous if she petted Flush. Poor Flush ! Browning that summer had clipped off all his curls to give him relief from heat and fleas. But he would happily race across the floor outdistancing Wiedeman when at Christmas time the baby began to creep, ready like Flush to rush for anything his parents would roll across the floor. He was an active child; yet he would sit on his mother's knee, listening quietly while his father played the piano, or wisely turning the pages of a book, putting up his little mouth for a kiss "every two minutes." Before he was a year old he was fast getting into mischief, "upsetting the water jugs till he is drenched (which charms him), pulling the broom to pieces, and having serious designs upon cutting up his frocks with a pair of scissors. He laughs like an imp when he can succeed in doing anything wrong." But, as his mother also wrote, "For my part and my husband's, we may be frank and say that we have caught up our parental pleasures with a sort of passion."

The deeper pleasure she found in her son the more Elizabeth's heart turned to her father. She worried over him when a cholera epidemic threatened London; she knew that he would not be persuaded either to leave town or to stay away from what she called "that horrid City"; then her sisters caused her anxiety by their report of their father's indisposition. She had continued to write to him never losing hope that in the end even if he did not forgive her, he would at least consent to see her and her son. In her letters she was careful not to argue with him about her conduct; she did not irritate him with the hint of a supposition that his severity to her had been more than justice. He himself had said to her sisters that this had been her only fault toward him; for this supposed fault she willingly asked his pardon. And she reiterated her love for him, love which was assuredly genuine. Since he did not now return her letters, she believed that he read them (though he never did) and she, with Browning's help, used every means to conciliate him. She told him that he need not openly forgive her; he need not before the world seem to condone her action. He could "act out his idea of justice" by excluding her and her child from any inheritance of his fortune. Then, having been just, he could afford to be merciful; he could grant her what she asked: forgiveness and affection. His silence remained unbroken.

Fortunately for her she found ample compensation in husband and child. Though she had been sceptical of married happiness, she found the years only deepening the love she felt for Browning and the adoration he felt for her. He wrote to Mrs. Jameson: "Ba must have told you about our babe, and the little else there is to tell — that is, for *her* to tell, for she is not likely to encroach upon *my* story which I *could* tell of her entirely angel nature, as divine a heart as God ever made; I know more of her every day; I, who thought I knew something of her five years ago !"

CHAPTER VIII

MARRIAGE with a poet had not, however, dimmed Elizabeth's devotion to poesy. Moreover her husband believed her a far greater poet than he could ever be himself; she, with a more exact critical power, placed him above herself. Yet had he been the lesser poet her critical powers would not have discerned his littleness, so far from conceit had she always been and so ready to look up to her menfolk. She had been fond of her sisters; her father and her brother Edward she had held to be of the stature of gods. Her estimate of Browning was different from the world's. At their marriage she was a poet of note; he an insignificant voice singing in the wilderness. English critics who piled the laurel crowns on her weak head seldom gave him a leaf of praise. They were more generous with their abuse.

Her poetry was constantly quoted, repeatedly included in anthologies. She was besieged with requests for autographs, consulted by budding poetesses, flattered by gentlemen who wrote long letters to tell her she was a muse. That these compilers and idolators passed over her better and simpler poems, preferring the more ambitious, less sincere, and more obscure made her the more scornful of them for rejecting her husband's verses as difficult.

And so vexation was mixed with her pleasure when at the death of Wordsworth she and not Browning was suggested for the vacant laureateship. Had their claims been put forward together she would have been happy; happy over the honor to them both; happy over the thought that she was, however unworthy, considered his equal. It did not please her to have her considered his superior, to have him wholly ignored, and herself proclaimed as a worthy candidate. Her friends wrote from England that London was agog with the rumor that she would be selected. The *Athenæum* gracefully stated her claim. It was felt that the selection of a woman — and of all the women writing verse Elizabeth was clearly the foremost — would be a delicate compliment to Queen Victoria. Her appointment might well have followed had it not been for the superior candidacy of Tennyson.

The discussion gave publicity to the new edition of her poems which contained revised versions of such of her two preceding volumes as she, or her publisher, thought worth preserving. She was not proud of her earlier poems, finding them full of "feeble rhymes, and turns of thought — such a dingy mistiness! Even Robert couldn't say a word for much of it." Yet the public had praised them. And she was not deaf to flattery.

In her private life there were still causes for unhappinesss. When, in March 1850, her sister Henrietta finally married her lovesick captain, Elizabeth's peace of mind was again troubled. Captain Surtees Cook, having at last achieved promotion and a livable though very modest income, had stormed the fortress of Mr. Barrett's obstinacy and had courageously asked for Henrietta's hand. He was told sternly what he already knew, that he had not sufficient money to maintain a wife properly. He was too fearful to suggest that a man of Mr. Barrett's wealth might subsidize his daughter. He learned, too, that his religious views were objectionable to Mr. Barrett. The interview, which had been hardly more than a monologue of Mr. Barrett's, ended with the statement that if Henrietta married it would be against her father's wishes, and he would never see her again.

Henrietta's resolution was nothing much to rely upon, but Captain Cook had already proved that persistence won; had he not sat out all other suitors and gained her consent to an engagement that had stood for five years? So now he set about working her up to the point of marriage. Her father, perhaps relying upon her known timidity and the captain's poverty, did not, as on previous occasions, make a tremendous scene. He had issued his orders. She had seen how firm he could be; he had banished Elizabeth when she disobeyed him, and he had not relented. Henrietta knew the penalty. She was no young girl, her head turned by a new lover; she knew this cousin as she knew her own brothers. She who had always lived in an ample household would not lightly face life on a narrow scale.

He misjudged both his own influence with his children and the determination of the captain. Henrietta defied him more openly than Elizabeth, publicly marrying her faithful lover in spite of her father's prohibition and her own lack of income. Ba had won happiness, and so should she.

Arabel remained at Wimpole Street, the only daughter Mr. Barrett now acknowledged, the only one whose name could be spoken in his presence. Elizabeth's reaction to the marriage was twofold. She rejoiced in Henrietta's happiness, hoping but not believing that it would parallel her own; she also felt that Henrietta's disobedience would by Mr. Barrett be laid at her door. She had shown the way, Henrietta had merely followed her down the path of sinful disobedience. Her own chances of being forgiven were therefore lessened. She would not go to England this year. Perhaps it was as well that they could not really afford the trip.

In the summer, a sharp attack of illness made her once more the centre of attention and withdrew her mind from brooding on her father's displeasure. Moreover, she took pride and comfort in the doctor's praise of a constitution that could so resist disease.

At Siena her health was completely restored and she could soon take walks with her husband. In a villa "set in the midst of its own vineyards and olive ground, apple trees and peach trees, not to speak of a little square garden," and magnificent views from all the windows, the Brownings lived frugally and happily. The baby, who had become pale in Florence, frightening his parents beyond measure when he suffered from sunstroke, grew rosy and merry.

Wiedeman at a year and a half was "a very curious

imaginative child, . . . too excitable for his age"; he was active of limb and in the main light-hearted. He would trot round the house singing little tunes of meaningless syllables. He did not deign to talk, preferring gestures which were easily understood by his parents, his nurse, and Wilson, in whose eyes he was always perfect. The child was highly imitative and unusually sympathetic. He would cry if Flush were so much as reprimanded; if his mother pricked her finger his tears flowed. He was extremely sensitive to beauty, being moved by music, or art, or architecture. He would kiss the angels in art-book pictures; he would scream in front of a church until his nurse took him in, where at the first note of the organ he would kneel. It amused his parents to see the tiny mite cross himself, fold his hands, and turn up his eyes as the hymns soared. His father declared that he would get his religious crisis over with his eyeteeth.

Anyhow, he was not yet ready to read the Bible which had been given him by the formidable Margaret Fuller who had turned up in Florence, astonishing the Brownings and the world by producing a husband, Marquis Ossoli, and a child already a year old. With the Brownings she and her gentle husband became friendly and with them they spent their last night in Italy, when the Bible was presented as a gift from their baby to the Brownings' baby. Margaret Fuller Ossoli herself wrote the inscription and strangely: "In memory of Angelo Eugene Ossoli." Jestingly she recalled a prophecy long since made to Marquis Ossoli "that he should shun the sea, for that it would be fatal to him"; yet she added that their ship was named the "Elizabeth" which she accepted as a good omen. From Gibraltar she wrote to Mrs. Browning telling of their being really embarked for America though not auspiciously since the ship's captain had died of small-pox. She had the misfortune to have the disease infect her own child, and the happiness to have him recover, before the final catastrophe in which she and her husband and child were drowned. Elizabeth was deeply touched; yet she felt that death might well have been kinder than life.

In Florence once more winter and spring slipped by. As usual the Brownings lived quietly, Browning having at marriage given up his participation in social life for which his wife had neither strength nor inclination. The exercise his vigorous constitution craved was supplied by long walks with Flush at his heel. Meanwhile, Elizabeth, black silk in this warmer land replacing the velvet of old, reclined on the sofa with her little son beside her. On the table at hand lay her small quill penholder and the small bits of paper upon which she still preferred to write. Her husband required seclusion for composition; she worked intently but casually. It did not disturb her to have Wiedeman on the couch with her or playing about the room. She would write as the mood came, never impatient of interruption. If visitors appeared she would tuck her papers unobtrusively in a book, picking up her work again when leisure offered. In general her mind worked in tiny cycles, much as she wrote in tiny hand on tiny papers. She liked things about her to be diminutive; she had her favorite editions of the classics in the smallest obtainable volumes. And she was inclined to work in small doses. Certainly no guest, however casual, ever felt that he was interrupting her.

In June 1851, the Brownings, faithful Wilson attending, set out on travels that were to keep them from their Florentine home for seventeen months. First they ventured to Venice where Elizabeth and the baby flourished while Browning grew melancholy and sleepless, and Wilson bilious. Wiedeman was in ecstasy over the churches, and, though he could not yet pronounce the word church in either Italian or English, he could and did chant whenever he saw one. And he would quaintly echo his parents' admiration of scenery — at least Wilson and Robert Browning declared his appreciation an echo; his mother believed it original.

After a month of Venice came Milan where Elizabeth climbed the three hundred and fifty steps to the top of the cathedral. Two days of Milan and then a journey through Switzerland, Elizabeth deeply moved by the grandeur which seemed "like standing in the presence of God when He is terrible."

Paris, of which Elizabeth had seen little in her flight five years before, pleased her as much as it did little Wiedeman — or Penini as he now came to be called from his own attempts to pronounce his name. He would embarrass Wilson by standing at the window of a print shop, roaring like the lions he saw pictured there. He would follow the balloon man till Wilson bought him balloons which, when they escaped from his fat fists, he would watch float away in the air, saying gravely that they were going to God Who "lives among the birds."

They left Paris reluctantly for London where for two months the Brownings rented an apartment at 26 Devonshire Street. They could not fail to be pleased by the recognition shown them both; their fellow-writers hastened to do them honor. Tennyson, himself abroad, begged them to make use of his house and servants. Had they not preferred simple quarters in London and a simple mode of living they could have taken their choice of the fine houses offered them, and have lived with their days and nights crowded with engagements.

Browning's chief joy was reunion with his father and sister, and their immediate whole-hearted appreciation of his wife, hitherto unknown to them. Elizabeth's joy was mixed. Arabel hastened to greet her, and devoted to her a great part of her time. Henrietta made a special journey to London to spend a week with her. Her brother Henry came to see her fairly often; three other brothers occasionally. Her brother George, who had been displeased over her elopement and had not relented before, now yielded as soon as he received from Robert Browning a letter that satisfied his pride. He now came to meet Browning, see Elizabeth, and pet Penini.

So far, Mr. Barrett had not been informed by anyone in his family of the presence in England of the Brownings. Mr. Kenyon advised Elizabeth not to write to him. Elizabeth, however, could not believe that he would remain obdurate when he knew that she was there with her child. She wrote him after the family had gone from London into the country — if she wrote before she was afraid that he might interfere with Arabel's daily visits to her. Not only did she write but Browning wrote, a letter so dispassionate, calm, reasoning, and conciliatory that when she read it she did not see how it could fail of effect. The only answer received by either was a "very violent and unsparing letter" to Robert Browning with which came unopened, the seals unbroken, all the letters which Elizabeth had written her father since her marriage. Mr. Barrett wrote that he regretted having been forced to keep them by him for lack of the proper address to which to return them. When Browning's mother had died Elizabeth, according to the custom of the times, had used black seals and black-edged envelopes. For all her father knew this might have indicated her husband's death; he did not even then break the seal.

Elizabeth knew now that she would never be forgiven. She thought that she could never write to him again. And yet she did write, three years later, when Mr. Barrett met with an accident that permanently lamed him. Though this letter was not returned to her, nor another later one, she had small hope of their having been read. The only notice which her father ever took of her was to pack Arabel and as many sons as possible off to the seashore or country whenever he heard of her being in London. Little Penini as he grew older became aware of his grandfather's inaccessibility, drawing the childish conclusion that his mother must have been very naughty to be so ignored. One day he thought the matter out:

"Mama, if you've been very, very naughty — if you've *broken china!* I advise you to go into the room and say, *'Papa, I'll be dood.'* "

On this first visit, however, the child was too young to notice much except the attention that was lavished upon him by his Browning relatives and by his Aunt Arabel. Then he was sufficiently grieved over the disappearance of Wilson, now his nurse and slave. Wilson, after nearly five years abroad, desired to spend two weeks with her family. At first Elizabeth had planned to send the child with her, but, finding that his presence would considerably interfere with Wilson's freedom and enjoyment, she undertook the care of the active two-year-old herself. As a result she had no time for poetry. The child, at first inconsolable over the loss of "Lily," soon transferred his tyranny to his mother who could scarce find time to write ten-page letters. She bathed him, dressed him, went walking with him, and slept with him in her arms. He was too fearful of her disappearance to play contentedly with other children or to be coaxed off by Arabel.

If she remained in London, thought Elizabeth, she might as well be nursemaid for she would never be poetess in such a climate. After two months her cough, though quieted, was not wholly conquered, and she grew constantly thinner. Visiting she would not go; nor would she revisit the scenes of her youth. Hope End she could have seen without distress, but it was too near Torquay; and there she could not go. The happiness of her marriage had not healed the wound of her brother's death.

Back to Paris went the Brownings where houses were less draughty and more compact, without the long frigid halls which in England threatened Elizabeth's life every time she went to a bedroom for a handkerchief. Moreover, the French had more luxurious sofas and armchairs. A sunny apartment banished the cough and once more Elizabeth gained strength for sightseeing.

It was in February 1852 that Elizabeth finally realized her ambition to meet George Sand. To escape the plague of her notoriety, George Sand had taken an assumed name, concealing as far as possible both this name and the place of her residence in Paris. For strangers to meet her was presumably impossible. Elizabeth, however, was determined. She had a letter of introduction from Mazzini; to this she appended a personal request for an interview coaxing her husband to add his signature to hers. These letters were entrusted to a friend who delivered them to a friend who delivered them to the famous and infamous authoress. The very next day Elizabeth received a kindly note appointing the hour for audience with the request that Browning accompany his wife. Though the weather was far too sharp for Elizabeth to venture out she represented to her husband the necessity for her going: "one might as well lose one's life as one's peace of mind forever, and if I lost seeing her I should with difficulty get over it. So I put on my respirator, smothered myself with furs, and, in a close carriage, did not run much risk after all."

George Sand, a large woman with glossy black hair and very white protruding teeth, received them with outstretched hand which Elizabeth would have kissed. "*Mais non, je ne veux pas,*" said George Sand, and kissed her admirer full on the mouth.

Except when she flashed her brilliant smile, George Sand seemed quite grave. This time there were present for her court only two or three young men all obviously dominated by her. Indeed, as Elizabeth remarked, it was George Sand who was the man in that company. Elizabeth soon saw her again, calling at her house one morning to find her surrounded by eight or nine men who sat in deferential silence when their oracle chose to talk. The oracle sat at a corner of the fireplace, calmly warming her feet, seeming to disdain her audience. Browning, though he did not approve her conduct, found her as interesting as did Elizabeth. He saw her more often, since he sometimes met her in his walks abroad. He did not demur at taking his wife to her rooms, in spite of the somewhat disreputable society to be found there: "crowds of ill-bred men who adore her *à genoux bas,* betwixt a puff of smoke and an ejection of saliva. Society of the ragged Red diluted with the lower theatrical. She herself so different, so apart, as alone in her melancholy disdain !" There was a Greek in Greek costume who used the familiar *tu* in speaking to her and who publicly kissed her — Elizabeth was not distressed though she was moved to a feeling of compassion toward George Sand, that "noble woman under the mud." There were other men who went down on their knees before her in that crowded room, shouting their admiration of her sublimity in the face of her quiet scorn. Elizabeth was disappointed in only one thing — she did not see George Sand smoke. She was as tolerant of this foible of the great authoress as she was forgiving of her morals; "the cigarette is really a feminine weapon if properly understood."

Next in importance to this meeting with George Sand was Elizabeth's visit to the theatre to see *La Dame aux Camélias* about the fiftieth night of its production. Elizabeth did not join the popular outcry of immorality; she considered the play both moral and human, though inexcusably tragic. The perfect acting made it exasperatingly real; there was "something profane in such familiar handling of life and death. Art has no business with real graveclothes when she wants tragic drapery. . ." There was much justice in the caricature displayed in the shop-windows — the audience in the pit protecting themselves "with multitudious umbrellas from the tears of the boxes." Robert Browning, for all his pretentions of blasé theatre-goer, cried almost as freely as Elizabeth whose theatrical days were few. At least the tears rolled down his cheeks, even though he did not feel his heart breaking as she did, or suffer a twenty-four-hour headache as the result of his sympathy.

In June it seemed safe for Elizabeth once more to brave the English climate. The Brownings were fellow guests with Walter Savage Landor at Mr. Kenyon's; they visited a neighbor of Charles Kingsley's and met that "Christian Socialist," finding him earnest, kindly, and delightfully genial. Tennyson announced the birth of his son and his delight in him in three letters to

Elizabeth; to Monckton Milnes' fashionable christening luncheon for his child she took Penini who looked very pretty and behaved beautifully except when he refused to kiss the baby because in its christening robes it was *"troppo grande."*

In spite of the pleasure and recognition England gave the Brownings, Elizabeth's cough was rapidly making London impossible, and in October her husband hurried her away. In Paris they watched the *coup d'état*, Elizabeth thrilled over her hero, Louis Napoleon. She imparted her enthusiasm to Penini who went about shouting lustily, *Vive Napoleon!* until the emperor himself heard and bowed. After such excitement Florence seemed quiet indeed.

Home in Italy, Elizabeth rested, watching her child grow, welcoming old friends, and working in her casual fashion on a new edition of her poems for which there was already a demand. In England she had had the pleasure of seeing her husband greeted by his more famous fellow poets as one of themselves; the public, however, was still lukewarm. The sales of his books remained negligible while three years had practically exhausted the revised edition of her poems. It was the blindness of the public she stressed, never her own popularity.

CHAPTER IX

AND NOW there came again in her life a deep
interest in spiritualism, the only subject upon
which she and her husband really disagreed.
They often had opposing political enthusiasms and ha-
treds, but the political situations changed with sufficient
rapidity to make their affiliations transient. They differed somewhat in their social code, Elizabeth being
more sympathetic toward lion-hunters than her more
vigorous husband. In these matters either might con-
vert the other — Elizabeth's gentle persistence usually
winning out. In the matter of spiritualism they remained
apart, Elizabeth credulous and her husband scornful, yet
each tolerant of the other's attitude.

The interest dated back to Harriet Martineau's mesmeric cure from cancer in 1844. Strong-minded masculine Miss Martineau was apparently doomed to painful
death when by means of mesmerism she was helped to
a swift recovery. Twice a day was she put into a mag-
netic trance; and soon she was buying bonnets and
parasols, astonishing her friends and neighbors by walking first one mile, then five miles a day. As she wrote
Elizabeth, whom she urged strongly to seek health by
the same means, she had regained her appetite and her
ability to sleep and was altogether a different person.
Not satisfied with pouring out her wonderful experience

to her numerous correspondents, Harriet Martineau pulled down a hornet's nest of controversy upon herself by publishing her tale in the *Athenæum* of November 23, 1844.

Miss Martineau, in reply to the insults heaped upon her for her credulity, said, in a private letter to Elizabeth, that she had feared the effect of publicity yet felt it her duty to suffer for the truth, sustained "by the recollection of Godiva." Elizabeth could not wholly approve of her publication since it was certainly vague and contradictory, being written from the point of view of enthusiasm rather than of reflective thinking.

The matter itself was puzzling. Miss Martineau had been invalided with no hope save for approaching death; she was better, incredibly better. Miss Mitford joined the believers, having a maid who readily fell in a trance, during which she could *"see behind her."* This Jane was mesmerized for deafness, and though her hearing did not improve, she served to show the marvellous powers of mesmerism. Miss Martineau's maid did more; she turned prophet and in a trance announced the wrecking of a vessel. Alas! unbelievers soon proved that she had been out in the town just before submittting to mesmerism, and the news of the wreck had already reached the town, though not her household. The *Athenæum* used this as if it were a complete exposure of mesmerism. Elizabeth, however, remarked shrewdly that it discredited mesmerism only in so far as that depended upon the truth of the wreck prophecy.

In the controversy which now raged, she took no active

part, in spite of an active interest, being friendly with Miss Martineau and Miss Mitford, and leaning toward credulity. She wrote: "I feel to be more and more standing on my head — which does not mean, . . . that I understand."

Here, she felt, was a phenomenon difficult to interpret. Intelligent people went to see Miss Martineau and her "apocalyptic" maid, and came away convinced. One man was sufficiently moved to drop upon his knees as he conversed with this untutored girl in Greek and Latin; while other people in the room at the time spoke to her in Latin, Italian, and German. When the mesmeriser touched the "organ of *imitation*" on the girl's head she translated into English what was said to her in any of five strange tongues; when he touched the "organ of *language*" she no longer translated, but answered in English whatever was said.

Miss Martineau, all belief and fired with missionary zeal, wrote again and again urging Elizabeth to send forthwith for a mesmeriser and be cured of her illness and weakness. But Elizabeth was not ready to take any such step. She had believed that this remedy would do her harm rather than good by overexciting her nervous system. Besides, her father was violently opposed to mesmerism. Elizabeth could never have dared send for a mesmeriser even had she chosen to risk the experiment on her health. In spite of her father, however, as she herself put it, she had "long been a believer." Harriet Martineau's experience certainly ought to establish the reality of mesmerism beyond reasonable doubt. To what else could one attribute the miracle of Harriet Martineau's health, she who had not owned a hat or a parasol, so sure it was that she would never be able to go out again, and who now walked five miles a day? And yet Elizabeth could not feel wholly convinced of her having been cured by mesmerism alone; she even wrote the possibility of doubt to Miss Martineau herself.

Though she disbelieved in mesmerisers, she did believe in mesmerism; she believed in it as something to be feared and dreaded; if there were anything in it, there must be a great deal. She wished indeed that she could disbelieve in its reality, so dreadful did its truth seem to her. She objected to "the subjection of the will and vital powers of one individual to those of another, to the extent of the apparent solution of the very identity." Her knowledge of it was not mere book knowledge; she had the direct testimony of Harriet Martineau in letters to herself; and she had the experience of her own sister. Her sister, less fearful and more eager of experience than Elizabeth, permitted herself to be mesmerised, falling into a trance during which, though she heard what was said about her, she could not open her eyes or speak. Whether or not she could have become a prophetess was never known; she did not try again because of Elizabeth's abhorrence. "Hideous and detestable," Elizabeth labelled the performance.

And yet belief was current. There sprang up a religious sect calling themselves "advocates of the 'third revelation'" who drew their whole system of theology from people in a trance.

Charlatans appeared everywhere to take advantage of the wave of credulity; and it was not long before one could buy prophecies and visions at so much an evening. In Paris the harvest was richer than in London; there the mesmerist did not even demand the presence of the person who would receive the prophecy. Give him but a lock of hair and he would work his marvels. Soon Elizabeth's sisters were receiving requests for locks of Elizabeth's hair to be sent to a Parisian mesmerist who had set up as oracle. Elizabeth's refusal was emphatic — and, fortunately, her sisters consulted her instead of stealing the lock. Had she yielded, she wrote, "I should have felt the steps of pale spirits treading as thick as snow all over my sofa and bed, by day and night, and pulling a corresponding lock of hair on my head at awful intervals. I, who was born with a double set of nerves, which are always out of order; the most excitable person in the world, and nearly the most superstitious. I should have been scarcely sane at the end of a fortnight !"

Miss Martineau had weathered the storm of criticism and had continued well, walking often fifteen miles a day, startling the world alike with her physical prowess and her suggestions for a feminine Parliament, before Elizabeth took up the matter with Browning, whose correspondence with her had begun just before Miss Martineau's miracle. The next year, finding Browning sceptic, Elizabeth sent him a large batch of books and letters from Harriet Martineau and from Edgar Allan Poe. Poe's account of a mesmeric experience, as contained in an article in an American magazine, was to

Elizabeth truly horrible. Though never fully convinced of all of Harriet Martineau's claims for mesmerism, Elizabeth nevertheless fully believed in mesmerism. She lent Browning Poe's poems, as well as the extract from the magazine, and Harriet Martineau's books that he might see what manner of writers these were who meddled with magic. Browning found Harriet Martineau's desire to inspire other maidservants to prophesy and other ladies to seek health by mesmerism, a subject for amusement rather than for credence. Yet he was not obstinate. He wrote to Elizabeth: "Understand that I do *not* disbelieve in Mesmerism — I only object to insufficient evidence being put forward as quite irrefragable. I keep an open sense on the subject — ready to be instructed; and should have refused such testimony as Miss Martineau's if it had been adduced in support of something I firmly believed. . ."

Their absorption in their own affairs led both Elizabeth and her lover away from mesmerism. Meanwhile, the vogue died with the forties until in the fifties a new marvel appeared in spiritualism. Table-rappings became as prominent as prophesying maidservants had been. Elizabeth's interest quickened. Mesmerism's workings she had viewed from the privacy of her room; as a recluse she had never actually seen the wonders. Now, though still frail, she was more of a normal woman, able to go about in the world, and hence able to view the phenomena of spiritualism at close range.

As she said of herself she was "a visionary . . . inclined to knock round at all the doors of the present world to try to get out"; she had once called herself nearly the most superstitious person in the world. She had at this time a large number of correspondents in America, and she frequently saw American magazines and newspapers. Spiritualism was rampant in and around Boston. Soon the fever had spread to Europe and in Florence as in Boston table-rapping séances were socially the rage. There were not, as supposed to be in America, fifteen thousand mediums, but there were great numbers of interested people who found table-moving more absorbing than whist.

The Browning home was not immune; when friends called, Elizabeth was eager to try the experiment. Early in the wave of credulity Elizabeth sat expectant with friends about her own table; and, though the experiment failed, her interest was not in the least dimmed. She explained the failure by the impatience of the group to have something happen at once; and by the presence of a sceptic — her own husband on this occasion played Mephistopheles. His sister in Paris shared his doubts, yet did not scorn to sit in at a private séance, refusing to be deeply impressed yet admitting that she saw no possibility of tricks having been played. At this séance the table, according to the approved style of the moment, answered according to the alphabet, rapping for each letter its number in the alphabet. The age of Penini was asked, and the table rapped correctly four times.

Elizabeth's interest deepened. She thoroughly enjoyed this new life of hers where she met people other than the adorers of her invalid days. She was fond of people, an eager listener, an enthusiastic talker. In Florence, she liked to have Browning gather about him in the evenings a group of men — writers, painters, sculptors — who would discuss life and literature, while she daringly permitted them to smoke cigars. Spiritualism absorbed these men almost as much as it did her. "Oh, we are believers here," she wrote, "except Robert, who persists in wearing a coat of respectable scepticism — so considered — though it is much out of elbows and ragged about the skirts. If I am right, you will none of you be able to disbelieve much longer. . . Imposture is absolutely out of the question, to speak generally; and unless you explain the phenomena by 'a personality unconsciously projected' (which requires explanation of itself), you must admit the spirit theory. As to the simpler forms of the manifestation (it is all one manifestation), the 'turning-tables,' I was convinced long . . . [ago] that *many* of the amateur performances were from involuntary muscular action — but what then ? These are only imitations of actual phenomena."

Such a faith was hard to disturb. Besides she had famous companions in her credulity: Longfellow's brother-in-law in Paris became so thoroughly interested as to give up his whole time and attention to an investigation of spiritualism. This Mr. Appleton was "still in doubt whether the intelligence is external, or whether the phenomena are not produced by an *unconscious projection in the medium of a second personality accompanied with clairvoyance, and attended by physical manifestations.*" Meanwhile, Mr. Appleton took to Lamartine's house, at the poet's request, a young American girl who was "a strong medium" as well as "a very sweet girl." Lamartine was delighted with the phenomena she produced, which included the spirit of Henry Clay declaring "*J'aime Lamartine.*" Louis Napoleon was reported to be guided by oracular raps, the Czar looked to tables for guidance, and the King of Holland forgot to rule and let himself be ruled by mediums.

All Elizabeth's friends and correspondents told her tales of the various and marvellous communications coming through. That many of the communications were excessively trivial did not at all disturb her faith. We are ourselves trivial, she said, and people did not always bring "serious souls and concentrated attentions and holy aspirations" to the waiting spirits. Besides death did not change people on the instant: "Foolish Jack Smith who died on Monday, is on Tuesday still foolish Jack Smith. If people who on Monday scorned his opinions prudently, will on Tuesday receive his least words as oracles, they very naturally go mad, or at least do something as foolish as their inspirer is. Also, it is no argument against any subject, that it drives people mad who suffer themselves to be absorbed in it. That would be an argument against all religion, and all love, by your leave. Ask the Commissioners of Lunacy; knock at the door of mad-houses in general, and inquire what two causes act almost universally in filling them. Answer — love and religion."

Though Browning was sceptic he was not uninterested. He was, however, somewhat perturbed over his frail wife's intensity of interest. She "sat in" at table experiments and was deeply impressed. She tried herself to do spirit-writing but though she felt the pencil turn in her hand, independent of her own volition, she did not have the power to write words or even letters. She kept up a correspondence with the friend of a friend, a woman who herself knew no Greek and yet who wrote Greek under a control. This mystical Greek she did not comprehend, but the beautifully written words were generally correct, Elizabeth said, "such words as 'Christ,' 'God,' 'tears,' 'blood,' 'tempest,' 'sea,' 'thunder,' 'calm,' 'morning,' 'sun,' 'joy.' No grammatical construction hitherto, but a significant sort of grouping of the separate words, as if the meaning were struggling into coherence. My idea is that she is being exercised in the language, in the *character,* in order to fuller expression hereafter."

Though credulous, Elizabeth, warned by her own common sense and the protecting protestations of her sensible husband, could not believe all the tales she heard, even though the letters that rained upon her swore that the phenomena were personally observed. She took their testimony with more than a grain of salt, finding much merriment in "visible spirit-hands, pianos playing themselves, and flesh-and-blood human beings floating about rooms in company with tables and lamps. Dante has pulled down his own picture from the wall of a friend of ours in Florence five times, signifying his pleasure that it should be destroyed at once as unauthentic (our friend burnt it directly . . .). Savonarola also has said one or two things, and there are gossiping guardian angels, of whom I need not speak." When the world got as mad as this there was naught for her to do but turn sensible and unbelieving. Here were her own trusted friends writing from London that they had shaken hands with spirits — "'softer, more thrilling than any woman's hand.'"

The Scotch-American medium Hume had now captured first London and then the continent. This young man for a time had the social and literary world at his feet. To his séances came notables and lordlings, all eager to feel spirit hands and to receive spirit messages. Though Mrs. Trollope withdrew her patronage after rumors of his peccadilloes in Florence, he was not at all perturbed, calmly making his way to Paris where he lived supposedly under the protection of the emperor. Hume it was who produced the manifestation of "two spiritual figures, male and female, who were *recognized* by their friends. Five or six persons (including the medium) fainted away at this apparition."

Hume was so successful in converting infidels to a belief in life after death that he expected to profit handsomely by their legacies, one Englishwoman promising him an annuity of two hundred and forty pounds. The Empress Eugénie showed her appreciation by acting as guardian of his little sister, educating the girl in Paris. He justified Elizabeth's faith in his virtue in spite of his obvious vanity and his known mistakes by returning to Italy to pay all his neglected debts.

In Rome during the winter of 1859, Elizabeth had much amusement in talking "with Theodore Parker, who believes nothing, . . . and has been writing a little Christmas book for the young just now, to prove how they should keep Christmas without a Christ, and a Mr. Hazard, a spiritualist, who believes everything, walks and talks with spirits, and impresses Robert with a sense of veracity, which is more remarkable." She took a fancy to this man Hazard whom Browning had presented to her as an intelligent and agreeable American, an opinion he did not reverse upon closer acquaintance and a knowledge of his calling. For Hazard was presumably no charlatan. He had made investigations for years, asserting a high motive, and had "seen the Impossible." In Elizabeth he found a most attentive listener.

Elizabeth argued that because one did not personally see anything in a half dozen experiments was no proof that there was nothing to be seen. She herself had not heard or read a single impressive communication. Nevertheless, she was immensely impressed with the fact that there were communications at all. Here were attested phenomena. What did they mean? What force was it that lifted Lord Lyndhurst in his chair ? What were the intelligences that framed the communications ? One never got anywhere by ignoring facts; these things were warranted genuine; then they were subjects for investigation. She felt that it was moral cowardice on Dickens' part to refuse his friends' pleas to join their investigations. Trollope, the writer, Chapman, the publisher, and Landseer, the artist, were all believers. Walter Savage Landor, however, was consistently scornful. He declared loftily to Elizabeth, with whom he was not at all sympathetic though he leaned heavily upon her husband, that he had "quite given up thinking of a future state — he had *had* thoughts of it once, but that was very early in life." Landor at this time having quarrelled with all the world except Robert Browning was permitting him to take care of him while he enjoyed life and his "most beautiful sea-foam of a beard . . . , all in a curl and white bubblement of beauty."

Landor might jeer and Dickens shut his eyes for all that Elizabeth cared. She read critically and carefully the English *Spiritual Magazine* to which she subscribed with her husband's permission.

Browning's objection to his wife's keen interest in spiritualism was never bigoted. He himself, though not denying that there might be some truth, was too impatient of sham to be imposed upon. Moreover, his wife's excitable nature, the eagerness with which she snatched at life, just as in her childhood she had uprooted potatoes and carrots impatient of their slow growth, an eagerness which thrust itself into the heart of the matter without having considered whether or not there were any matter to have need of investigation, this made it advisable for him to cool her ardor. He might well for her sake have feigned an indifference he did not feel; actually however, his feet remained on solid ground throughout all the miracle-working and ghost-walking. So long as he was with her to prevent any undue excitement, any unreflective foolishness, he indulged her as always. Years later he presented in *Sludge the Medium* his own attitude and what he presumed to be that of the medium, Hume. He lets Sludge present his own case, Sludge who from poor, ill-fed outcast became society's darling. Who could blame him for juggling a little to let his benefactors have the manifestations they craved from the spirit world ? Browning could not, like his wife, divorce spiritualism from the mediums responsible for it; he could not believe it better than its practitioners, though his wife assured him ten times over that fraudulent mediums did not invalidate the truth of their findings. In his poem *Mesmerism* he presents a medium summoning a spirit not for the amusement of the idle rich, but for his own love's sake:

> . . . since eve drew in, I say,
>   I have sat and brought
>   (So to speak) my thought
> To bear on the woman away,
> Till I felt my hair turn grey —
>
> Till I seemed to have and hold,
>   In the vacancy
>   'Twixt the wall and me,
> From the hair-plait's chestnut-gold
> To the foot in its muslin fold —
>
> Have and hold, then and there,
>   Her, from head to foot,
>   Breathing and mute,
> Passive and yet aware,
> In the grasp of my steady stare —
>
>   .   .   .
>
> On doth she march and on
>   To the fancied shape;
>   It is, past escape,
> Herself, now: the dream is done
> And the shadow and she are one.

First I will pray. Do Thou
    That ownest the soul,
    Yet wilt grant control
To another, nor disallow
For a time, restrain me now!

I admonish me while I may,
    Not to squander guilt,
    Since require Thou wilt
At my hand its price one day!
What the price is, who can say?

This was very much Elizabeth's point of view — a horror that one's soul could be controlled by another; that human beings alive or dead should be subject to the will of medium or mesmerist. Browning, though fundamentally sceptical, recognized some truth in this groping after spirit language. His life and Elizabeth's were too closely knit for him to ignore her beliefs; moreover, their close association had led to many a telepathic communication. In *By the Fireside* Browning represents himself watching silently his wife

Reading by fire-light, that great brow
    And the spirit-small hand propping it,
Mutely, my heart knows how —

When, if I think but deep enough,
    You are wont to answer, prompt as rhyme;
And you, too, find without a rebuff
    The response your soul seeks many a time
Piercing its fine flesh-stuff.

It was because of this close sympathy that Browning yielded to his wife's desire to investigate spiritualism with her enthusiastic thoroughness. She pleaded with her friends who attended séances in London and in Paris to send her all details. Her husband had confidence in her ultimate steadiness to protect her from any danger-ous or embarrassing entanglements. She had said sin-cerely, "I have no more confidence, apart from my own conscience and discretionary selection, in spirits out of the body than in those embodied." She would, she de-clared, as willingly take her theology from the pope as from the spirits. And when she found her friends yield-ing to the dictation of spirits she urged them vehemently to throw off such a yoke and assert their own individu-ality.

Her desire was to *know* more of everything in and out of the world. Her own experience had been narrow in-deed until she had married. As wife and mother she had enlarged her experiences, and by travel and social contacts she had enlarged her horizon. Even so it was a limited view that she could have of the world. Her husband was ever at her side, her strength was never normal, and a large part of her life was still lived by her own fireside. So she sent her mind wandering. She peered into the world of spirits, believing it an extension of the everyday world.

It was this ability to project herself into experiences other than her own that produced the loveliness of *A Musical Instrument* when in spirit she actually saw Pan, heard the whispering of the reeds, saw the golden glint on the river, and understood the beauty and the pathos of the music he made. Perhaps the Victorian reader who lost his admiration for her (as he wrote her anonymously and vituperatingly) because of this "immoral" poem was its most acute reader, since he obviously sensed the identification of the poet with the great god Pan.

And it was her sheltered life that sent her mind wandering, though somewhat delicately, in brothels in *Aurora Leigh* and in wicked high society in *Lord Walter's Wife* which Thackeray felt obliged to reject when she sent it to the *Cornhill Magazine*. Elizabeth believed that the society of the day (of which she had the meagerest experience) was sadly corrupt. She had a naïve interest in its vices; and she liked to think that her interest was due to a desire to mend by chiding. She believed that while pure women chose to ignore vice, miserable women would continue to suffer wrong.

Had Thackeray scored the poem on the grounds of its being doggerel he might have had less need of tact and been much nearer the truth. The poem deals with an engaged man's love for a married wife and mother who turns the tables on him rather clumsily. Elizabeth enjoyed picturing the scene in which a pure woman pretended to be "vile" — which meant that she would deceive her husband and receive the attentions of the other man under the eyes of her little daughter — in order to pour scorn upon the man when he dared not take her at her word. Thackeray mulled over the poem for months, not daring to print it, and not wishing to hurt Elizabeth's feelings by his refusal. Finally he achieved a most tactful letter, saying in part: "You see that our *Magazine* is written not only for men and women but for boys, girls, infants, sucklings almost, and one of the best wives, mothers, women in the world writes some verses which I feel certain would be objected to by many of our readers. Not that the writer is not pure, and the moral most pure, chaste, and right, but there are things *my* squeamish public will not hear on Monday, though on Sundays they listen to them without scruple. In your poem, you know, there is an account of unlawful passion, felt by a man for a woman, and though you write pure doctrine, and real modesty, and pure ethics, I am sure our readers would make an outcry, and so I have not published this poem."

Thackeray's rejection of the poem did not hurt Elizabeth's pride, nor did it divert her poetry into other channels.

CHAPTER X

I N WRITING *Aurora Leigh,* Elizabeth was gratifying a long-felt desire. Years before she had meditated a poetical autobiography; and again and again the idea had beset her to write a novel in rhyme. From her invalid's seclusion she might have published a slightly veiled autobiography since the world knew little of her personally and would not be able to break in upon her to verify details. However, she worked slowly; and the years were taken up with learned reading, with essay writing for Horne, with letters, and with less ambitious poems. Then came the startling change in her life when new scenes and the intoxication of fulfilled love kept her completely occupied. Hence it was not until her little son was well past infancy that she began to work out her idea.

Even then she did not work at it with any degree of intensity. There were so many diversions in this new life that she accomplished no more with her increased strength. Besides there was Penini, himself an occupation even before it became necessary to teach him to read and write, or to choose carefully his beruffled frocks. Elizabeth herself gave him his daily lessons, no small task since the child was taught to read in French, English, and Italian; and his father taught him music when he got beyond the stage of desiring to accompany his father's fugues with two or three drums.

Penini wrote poems, too, which were seemingly far more important than any of his mother's. And he fell prey to fever now and again — once in Rome he was frighteningly ill. His mother could not divorce her thoughts from him even in health.

But, fortunately, she was one who could work amid many interruptions, placidly setting aside her writing and taking it up again when occasion offered, apparently at will summoning the necessary absorption and intensity. Whatever she did was done with her whole heart and soul; she was never one to skim lightly over any experience. And she continued to take her poetry with the same seriousness that she took Penini, Italian politics, and spiritualism. If, when her trunk was missent, she worried more over Penini's flounced garments than over the manuscript of the first part of *Aurora Leigh* it was because the need for the child's finery was immediate — she wished him to appear his prettiest before Parisian and London friends. There was no hurry for the poem; and if it should be lost it could be more easily reconstructed than the boy's wardrobe. She could not sew; she could write poetry.

She was far from undervaluing *Aurora Leigh* which in her dedication to John Kenyon she called the most mature of her works, the one in which her "highest convictions upon Life and Art" were expressed; but she overvalued the appearance of Penini who, long after other boys were happily in trousers, went about clad in velvet and laces, with long golden curls framing his sensitive face. So proud of him was she that she kept him with her when celebrities came for an evening; and ten o'clock would find the boy prettier than ever with the flush of weariness and excitement.

So *Aurora Leigh* was of secondary importance during the three years of its composition. Elizabeth's preceding publication *Casa Guidi Windows* had not been a success. She published it at a time when she was visiting in France and England, and had expected it to attract attention, even to make a bit of a martyr of her. She thought it possible that she might not be allowed back into Italy because of her frank opinions on Italian affairs. But Italians did not read English poems though their author lived among them; and the English public did not by any means share Elizabeth's ideas of the importance of Italian liberty. The petty revolutions and squabbles which seemed to her, as an onlooker, thrilling; the backsliding which seemed to her tragic, were to her insular countrymen all in a day's work. Her poem, the understanding of which depended upon a rather erudite knowledge of Italian history, fell unnoticed in the year's literary scrap-basket. What attention it got was distinctly unfavorable. For the sake of a few fine lines no one wanted to plough through dull pages.

Since, however, Elizabeth wrote not for appreciation but because of a desire to serve Poetry she was not daunted. After all *Casa Guidi Windows* was merely a woman's expression of a woman's viewpoint; and this was a man's world. Men did not want women meddling with their politics. They were willing to let her meddle with their world of love.

ELIZABETH BARRETT BARRETT AS A CHILD
Reprinted with the permission of the Bibliophile Society

PENINI IN 1859, TEN YEARS OLD
Reprinted with the permission of Miss Lillian Whiting

And *Aurora Leigh* is a love story. It is a highly romantic story as turgid and as daring as *Jane Eyre* from which it borrows occasionally tone and incident. Part of it is autobiographical since the heroine is a writer entirely devoted to her art, believing herself immune to love. Here, however, the resemblance between Elizabeth and Aurora ends save as Aurora's sentiments gibe with her author's. Their views are frequently identical; their outward lives differ widely after childhood. Aurora, like Elizabeth, was bred in a remote country estate. Their condition was, nevertheless, different even then, Aurora being the temperamental child of an austere Englishman and a Florentine mother who died when she was four years old. Aurora, at her father's death when she was thirteen, was sent to England to the charge of an unloving aunt, her father's sister, a strait-laced woman, fearing all emotion, except hate. Hate she still cherished for the child's Italian mother who had robbed England of her brother.

> She had lived, we'll say,
> A harmless life, she called a virtuous life,
> A quiet life, which was not life at all
> (But that, she had not lived enough to know),
> Between the vicar and the country squires,
> The lord-lieutenant looking down sometimes
> From the empyrean to assure their souls
> Against chance-vulgarisms, and, in the abyss
> The apothecary, looked on once a year
> To prove their soundness of humility.
> The poor-club exercised her Christian gifts
> Of knitting stockings, stitching petticoats,
> Because we are of one flesh after all

And need one flannel (with a proper sense
Of difference in the quality) — and still
The book-club, guarded from your modern trick
Of shaking dangerous questions from the crease,
Preserved her intellectual. She had lived
A sort of cage-bird life, born in a cage,
Accounting that to leap from perch to perch
Was act and joy enough for any bird.
Dear heaven, how silly are the things that live
In thickets, and eat berries !

The excellent, restrained, ironical portrait of this woman pleased Victorians who knew her counterpart — there was one in every family. Elizabeth may well have drawn her by considering her sister Arabel, leaving out Arabel's sweetness. Arabel had not escaped from home; she had not followed Elizabeth, Henrietta, and Alfred into the exile of matrimony. She had stayed in her cage, seeking outlet for her emotions in charities and poor-schools. Elizabeth contemplated her narrow life and saw what she might have been with a less generous nature. Having fashioned her fictitious character she pictured her thoroughly. This elderly English maiden did her duty toward her orphan niece, smoothing her "copious curls" into neat braids, teaching her the catechism and the ways of English children:

She liked a woman to be womanly,
And English women, she thanked God and sighed
(Some people always sigh in thanking God),
Were models to the universe.

So Aurora had to tame her Tuscan ways, learn cross-stitch, model flowers in wax, spin glass, paint pretty water-color landscapes, draw neatly draped nereids, and perform prodigies of tinkling on the piano. For reading matter she was given books on womanhood, books that showed how fine it was for maidens to abjure thinking, to echo the world — and husbands when they acquired them — and to sit peaceably sewing without a glance at the world of men.

Such an education Elizabeth had not been subjected to herself. Her scorn of it was, then, partly her scorn for the women who were products of such a system.

Aurora romantically drooped hoping and believing that she would soon find release in death. Her cousin Romney, who conveniently lived on the adjoining estate, taunted her with this desire for release until she came no longer to desire it. Finding relief in her father's books and a secret intellectual life, she poured out her soul in interminable verses, and nevertheless blossomed into an attractive young lady whom Romney sought in marriage. Romney had no admiration for her verses which against her will he had read; he was himself a visionary of a different stamp, one afire with humanitarian zeal. He tried to convince his cousin that women were weak in art, strong in duty. Aurora, however, was no meek damsel to be dazzled by the offer of a man's hand and the thought of helping suffering humanity. Woman, she declared hotly, was not the mere complement of man. Social theory was already Romney's wife; why should he look beyond ?

Romney carried her refusal to her aunt, telling how he had lost his suit because he had asked for a helpmeet

instead of babbling incoherently of love. The old lady's
scorn struck swiftly:

> . . . are they queens, these girls ?
> They must have mantles, stitched with twenty silks,
>   Spread out upon the ground, before they'll step
>   One footstep for the noblest lover born.

In vain did Aurora plead that her path was that of art,
not love. She had no choice, her aunt said; she was a
beggar. Her father had indeed been rich; but he had
lost the right to leave his property to any child of his;
he had not thought of sons or daughters when he fell in
love; nor of that clause in the entail that excluded off-
spring by a foreign wife,

> (The clause set up a hundred years ago
> By a Leigh who wedded a French dancing-girl
> And had his heart danced over in return).

Aurora was dependent upon the bounty of her aunt
whose death would leave her all but penniless since the
estate reverted to Romney. This, far from throwing a
repentant girl upon Romney's charity, stirred up the hot
Italian blood to firmer resistance. Six weeks she lived
in a dazed silence, conscious of the very servants' intensity
of interest. Then suddenly her aunt died. Like the
noblest of romantic heroes Romney tried to give Aurora
a legacy. Less generous than he, Aurora refused the gift
and with her small wealth departed to win fame for herself as a writer.

Aurora, successful, led a life empty of practically everything save devotion to her art. Her mail — like Eliza-

beth's own — was full of requests for autographs and interviews, the silly admiration of unthinking people. The
critics treated her now well, now ill, the excellent things
which she did indifferently being less praised than the
bad she did excellently. Spiritually she lived by verse
but since

> In England no one lives by verse that lives;

she had recourse to prose to earn her bread. In all the
world's praise she missed Romney's; he did not write;
she wondered if he even read her books. News of him
came somewhat abruptly when the beautiful high-born
Lady Waldemar called upon her. Lady Waldemar declared herself deeply in love with Romney who, unmindful of her wishes, spent his time, energy, and money upon
the poor in a dream of human brotherhood. She came
to enlist Aurora's help. For Romney, quixotic in all
things, had determined to marry a girl of the people, one
Marian Erle. To save him from this error the proud
lady had come to Aurora.

Perhaps from curiosity, perhaps from a desire to please
Romney, more likely from a need to see what manner
of girl this was who would take her cousin from her
forever, Aurora wended her way through alleys and
mean streets and climbed to Marian's garret, finding
there a sweet, pretty maid, devotedly in love with the
gentleman who had rescued her from an impossible life.
In developing Marian's tale, Elizabeth had a chance to
wallow in all the mud which her own feet had never
once approached. The more sheltered her own life, the

more dreadful must be that of unprotected girls. Herself untempted, she gained the thrill of temptation in contemplating what might have happened had she been low-born. Marian was the child of unlovely tramps from whom she would steal to gaze upon the beauty of sky and country. In contrast to her brawling parents, she was quiet and meditative, reading everything she could get — odd pages loosened from books which good-natured pedlars would give her. She went to Sunday-school, too, and learned about God. She was industrious and earned a few pence in each village they passed through by mending and knitting hose. Her parents when drunk would beat her, and for the rest ignore her; until one dreadful day when her mother, having herself been beaten overmuch, seized upon her, loosened her thick long hair and led her to the squire, who willingly paid a good price for the girl. Mere child that she was Marian knew right from wrong; with a fearful shriek she loosed her mother's grasp and fled. She ran until she fainted. A friendly carter coming upon her thus, conveyed her to a convalescent home. After an appropriately long fever, Marian recovered. Romney, the protector of the poor and oppressed, found her honorable employment. She worshipped her rescuer though she did not see him again for a year, when he found her nursing a dying girl whom all had deserted. It was then, in view of her self-sacrificing sweetness, that Romney proposed in a manner reminiscent of Jane Eyre's Mr. Rochester. God made them of one clay, said Romney; he "born what men call noble" and she "issued from the noble people" stood "at the two extremes of social classes."

In Marian's garret chamber Romney and Aurora met for the first time since their parting in the magnificence of Leigh Hall. Aurora kindly patted Marian upon the head and told Romney that she was a good girl. She went further and asked that the marriage be celebrated from her home — but no, Romney was determined to take his bride from "the people." A magnificent wedding he arranged in London's most fashionable church a month hence; to it he invited rabble and lordlings equally; and all came, even Aurora who in the meantime had not been kind enough to see Marian again. Lady Waldemar had been more attentive.

The scene at the church Elizabeth lingered over — fine gentlemen talking superciliously and haughtily, curious ladies gabbling gossip, the riffraff of London talking as she imagined they must from her vast acquaintance with them — in Dickens' novels. When Marian failed to appear and the audience grew restive, a rough man cried out:

> "Now, look to it, coves, that all the beef and drink
> Be not filched from us like the other fun,
> For beer's spilt easier than a woman's lost!"

and a woman shrieked:

> "I'm a tender soul,
> I never banged a child at two years old
> And drew blood from him, but I sobbed for it
> Next moment, — and I've had a plague of seven.

This woman went on to accuse Romney of having meant no good to the girl; fine gentry overcome girls by promising wedding rings

> ". . . and then . . .
> A choking finger on her throat last night,
> And just a clever tale to keep us still,
> As she is, a poor lost innocent."

At this the mob took up the cry, "the girl, the girl!" and riot broke loose. Here Aurora conveniently fainted, thus making it unnecessary to describe a scene of which Elizabeth could not be sure.

After a long digression in which Aurora discussed herself and her devotion to art, the narrative winds back to Romney Leigh and Marian two years later. Romney had converted Leigh Hall into almshouses. Aurora had the news at a fashionable gathering where she overheard young men make lascivious remarks. Looking toward Lady Waldemar one youth "with low carnivorous laugh" called her a flower:

> She neither sews nor spins, — and takes no thought
> Of her garments . . . falling off.

Ladies used to have in their gowns too much starch; now it was too little lawn. When the young man went on to such expressions as "prejudice of sex" his elder companion thought fit to reprove him, thereby bringing out an unusual train of thought for any Victorian, a defence of the younger generation:

The young run on before, and see the thing
That's coming. Reverence for the young, I cry.
In that new church for which the world's near ripe,
You'll have the younger in the Elder's chair,
Presiding with his ivory front of hope
O'er foreheads clawed by cruel carrion-birds
Of life's experience.

Somewhat outspoken — for Victorian literature — was
the older man's reply:

> "I plucked
> A silver hair this morning from my beard,
> Which left me your inferior. Would I were
> Eighteen and worthy to admonish you !
> If young men of your order run before
> To see such sights as sexual prejudice
> And marriage-law dissolved, — in plainer words,
> A general concubinage expressed
> In a universal pruriency, — the thing
> Is scarce worth running fast for, and you'd gain
> By loitering with your elders."

Such language Elizabeth, as a married woman, felt free
to use, though she thereby startled her readers; such
words really ought not to have been in a lady's vocabulary. More startling than such conversation to Aurora
was the news that Romney Leigh was to marry Lady
Waldemar. This was somehow torture to her. She
wrote a scathing letter to the Lady, safe from reply since
she that instant decided to leave England. Romney had
loved her, she knew; could he now love this false
woman ?

Paris brought further melodrama when in a crowded
street Aurora caught a glimpse of Marian, unmistak-

ably she, a baby under her shawl. By haunting the streets the poet finally found her again and learned her sad history. Lady Waldemar was the villain of the piece as might have been suspected. She had visited Marian during the engagement to Romney, had flattered the girl, had worked upon her emotions until she made her see that it was her duty to give Romney up. Adoring him, Marian could see no way out save flight. If she must lose this dream of happiness, she must go secretly, for she never could resist him if he refused her sacrifice. Lady Waldemar arranged all; Marian would go to Australia with a former maid of hers whom she trusted.

The traditions of melodrama demanded that her trust be betrayed. Marian was taken to France, drugged, and seduced. Waking in the morning half-mad when she knew her betrayal, she fled, seeking safety anywhere. After many vicissitudes she took service as a maid, finding dull oblivion in work until her mistress one day reviled her and sent her adrift. She had not known that she was to have a child. Here in Paris she showed her beautiful year-old boy to Aurora who quickly repented her reproaches, remaining to adore the infant. Having wronged Marian by her first suspicion of her lightness, she decided instantly to make reparation by adopting mother and child. To Florence they went where Marian, seeing her baby thrive, grew happy; even alone with him in France she had been careful always to show a smiling face that he might grow up in a joyful world never knowing the sorrows that had been hers.

To them came news of Romney's difficulties with his rabble that, unappreciative of his devotion, had burned Leigh Hall. Soon after came Romney himself to talk high-mindedly with Aurora, who fenced, thinking him on his honeymoon with Lady Waldemar. After whole pages of misunderstandings she learned two things — first, that he was not married and had come to wed Marian and adopt her baseborn child. When Marian nobly rejected his offer in order to dedicate her life to her little son, never displacing him with other children, Aurora learned the second truth about Romney — that she loved him. Now that she found him blind (the fact had not been apparent to her in spite of his gropings) she loosed her emotions and yielded to her love. So, like Rochester in *Jane Eyre,* Romney had to give up his eyes to win his true love.

Elizabeth was, however, perturbed when a friend reminded her that she had taken her catastrophe from *Jane Eyre.* She sent to the library for the book at once, to refresh her memory. Meanwhile she assured her correspondent that the resemblance must be slight. Rochester was "monstrously disfigured and blinded in a fire . . . and the circumstance of his being hideously scarred is the thing impressed chiefly on the reader's mind. Now if you read over again those pages of my poem, you will find that the only injury received by Romney in the fire was a blow and from the emotion produced by the *circumstances* of the fire. Not only did he *not* lose his eyes in the fire, but he describes the ruin of his house as no blind man could. . . Afterwards he had a fever, and the eyes, the visual nerve, perished, showing no external stain — perished as Milton's did. I believe that a great shock on the nerves might produce such an effect in certain constitutions, and the reader on referring as far back as Marian's letter (when she avoided the marriage) may observe that his eyes had never been strong, that her desire had been to read his notes at night, and save them. For it was necessary, I thought, to the bringing-out of my thought, that Romney should be mulcted in his natural sight."

Rochester's accident was merely the prelude to wedding bells, Romney's had "metaphysical intention." Elizabeth explained patiently, pained that her readers did not immediately understand: "Romney had to be blinded, observe, to be made to see; just as Marian had to be dragged through the uttermost debasement of circumstances to arrive at the sentiment of personal dignity."

Moreover the poem was a defence of women's mental abilities and independence. Tennyson's *Princess* some years before had told a story in rhyme, but hardly a story of such weight as *Aurora Leigh;* his was a light tale lightly told, not exactly complimentary to women. Tennyson's heroine having tried an intellectual experiment, yielded to the first masculine onslaught. Aurora Leigh having climbed to success and fame yielded to love only when she had undeniably reached her goal and her suitor had pathetically failed to reach his.

To Elizabeth the ideas behind the story were the important part of the poem. But the general public saw little beyond a melodramatic romance, a novel in verse which was easily read, easily understood, and which was vastly entertaining. When criticisms appeared branding Aurora "a brazen-faced woman" and the story a grossly indecent romance the public grew even more appreciative. Mothers took to forbidding the book to their daughters, which, Elizabeth realized, was the best way to insure their reading it. Ladies of sixty wrote letters to the editor and to the poet that they "never felt themselves pure since reading it." The *National Magazine* printed a cartoon representing the author of *Aurora Leigh* with "the head of a 'strong-minded giantess' on the neck of a bull." Elizabeth's small son Penini looking upon the cartoon declared hotly: "It's not a bit like; it's too old, and *not half so pretty.*"

Browning, however, was not amused. He was given to immoderate anger at all times over any adverse criticism of his wife. A few years later when she was no longer present to restrain him he gave full vent to his fury. Edward Fitzgerald, literary recluse, whose translation of the *Rubaiyat* had found the public unappreciative, had flippantly remarked at Elizabeth's death, "Thank God, we'll have no more *Aurora Leigh's!*" Fitzgerald had already followed Elizabeth into the next world when Browning learned of this exclamation and flung after him a glass of vitriol:

I chanced upon a new book yesterday:
I opened it, and where my fingers lay
    'Twixt page and uncut page these words I read —
Some six or seven at most — and learned thereby

That you, Fitzgerald, whom by ear and eye
   She never knew, "Thanked God my wife was dead."
Ay, dead ! and were yourself alive, good Fitz,
How to return you thanks would task my wits.
   Kicking you seems the common lot of curs —
While more appropriate greeting lends you grace;
Surely to spit there glorifies your face —
   Spitting from lips once sanctified by hers.

The public did not share Fitzgerald's low opinion of *Aurora Leigh* which almost instantly became the book of the hour. In two weeks the first edition was exhausted; a second and a third followed and in two years there was demand for a fourth edition. Browning genuinely wished that he might have been its author, that he might have had the joy of showing it to his wife as his work. Other poets, not blinded by personal love, were equally mistaken in their estimation of *Aurora Leigh*. Poets and professional critics vied with one another for superlatives. Barry Cornwall called it "a hundred times over, the finest poem ever written by a woman." Walter Savage Landor wrote, "there is the wild imagination of Shakespeare. . . I had no idea that anyone in this age was capable of so much poetry. I am half drunk with it." Ruskin told the public: "Mrs. Browning's *Aurora Leigh* is, as far as I know, the greatest poem which the century has produced in any language," while he grew even more emphatic as he dilated on the subject in a personal letter to Robert Browning: "I think *Aurora Leigh* the greatest *poem* in the English language, unsurpassed by anything but Shakespeare —

not surpassed by Shakespeare's *Sonnets,* and therefore the greatest poem in the language."

The success of *Aurora Leigh* did not make Elizabeth vain. Penini, as she herself said, was more to her than twenty Aurora's. Her joy in its completion was much clouded, and her pleasure over its success much dimmed because the good friend to whom it was dedicated did not live to share her triumph. John Kenyon died in December 1856, soon after the book's appearance. He had been ill for a long time, and the Brownings' anxiety had been great during their visit in England that summer.

In spite of many pleasures the stay in England was on the whole painful to Elizabeth; in the first place her sister Henrietta had been unable, for lack of funds, to come to London, and for the same reason the Brownings had been unable to visit her. Then soon after their arrival Arabel had been spirited away to the Isle of Wight —Mr. Barrett's only notice of his errant daughter's presence in England. Thither, however, the Brownings followed her, spending some time with her before going to the other end of the island to console the dying Kenyon. On the island Penini, to his mother's amusement, was converted into an English boy by "mine untles."

There were other amusements, too. The literati crowded round the Brownings, taking more of their time than they could afford since both poets had works to see through the press.

"One of the pleasantest things which has happened to us here is the coming down on us of the Laureate, who, being in London for three or four days . . . , spent two of them with us, dined with us, smoked with us, opened his heart to us (and the second bottle of port), and ended by reading *Maud* through from end to end, and going away at half-past two in the morning. If I had a heart to spare, certainly he would have won mine. He is captivating with his frankness, confidingness, and unexampled *naïveté !* Think of his stopping in *Maud* every now and then — 'There's a wonderful touch ! That's very tender. How beautiful that is !' Yes, and it *was* wonderful, tender, beautiful, and he read exquisitely in a voice like an organ, rather music than speech."

But Elizabeth had been glad to leave England to return to the quiet of Italy. In the letters which followed her, praising *Aurora,* there was sometimes pleasure, sometimes pain. Ruskin's extravagant praise had rather embarrassed her; she was far more delighted when his next letter praised Browning:

"You please me — oh, so much — by the word about my husband. When you wrote to praise my poems, of course I had to bear it — I couldn't turn round and say, 'Well, and why don't you praise him, who is worth twenty of me ? Praise my second Me, as well as my Me proper, if you please.' One's forced to be rather decent and modest for one's husband as well as for one's self, even if it's harder. I couldn't pull at your coat to read *Pippa Passes,* for instance. I can't now."

This was not posing; it was the sincerity of a devoted wife and a sane critic. Browning was misled by his love to rate her poetry far above his own; she saw more truly that beside his organ hers was but a tinkling cymbal. His was the deeper knowledge of men and motives; even in these years of freedom her vistas had never been large. Her first-hand knowledge of different kinds of people was extremely limited. In her travels she was carefully protected; often confined to the house upon her arrival in strange cities. She received company, but hardly a motley crowd. As the years went on and she approached fifty, often a difficult age for women, her strength became less, and more and more the winters, in spite of change to softer climates, turned her into a semi-invalid clinging to the fireside.

Browning, in the meantime, lived in the world. He went to dinners and parties, often making his engagements three deep of an evening. His wife, knowing how much he depended upon people for occupation, encouraged him to such gaieties; it was no part of her nature selfishly to deprive him of what she could not herself have. Her husband had no "office" to go to so many hours a day; he had no fixed occupation. Poesy was, to be sure, an exacting mistress, but her demands were never constant. After an attempted piece of work was finished (and during its progress four hours a day were usually all that could profitably be given to it); a poet needed change and recreation. Days had many hours — Browning could fill some of them with walks, with Penini's music lessons, with his own playing, with his wife; but evening came and he needed the diversion which society could best give him. So in Rome whither they went for the winter Browning was gay. "Dissipations decidedly agree with Robert," wrote Elizabeth, "there's no denying that, though he's horribly hypocritical, and 'prefers an evening with me at home,' which has grown to be a kind of dissipation also." She encouraged him to go out though his going meant for her long lonely evenings to be filled with letter-writing and such books as the lean libraries and shops of Rome could furnish. She would creep early to bed, to rest against the occupations of the days — Penini's lessons were still in her hands. The child was now reading aloud to his mother an Italian translation of *Monte Cristo,* his first novel, to which he gave passionate allegiance, announcing solemnly at break-fast that for the future he meant to read novels, all Dumas to begin with and then his father's favorite book, *Madame Bovary!* "Heavens," wrote his proud mother, "what a lion-cub! Robert and I could only answer by a burst of laughter. It was so funny, that little dot of nine and a half full of such hereditary tendencies.

"And *Madame Bovary* in a course of education!"

Penini had progressed beyond the days when he had learned his lessons on his mother's lap, she holding the restless arms and legs and bribing him to gain a few moments' attention. Now he kept his bedside candle burning and read till he could no longer hold his eyes open. He was a tense little boy, taking life as seriously and emotionally as his mother. An ardent Italian, he shared his mother's political loves and hates, and with her he adored Louis Napoleon.

And yet for all his oddities he was much of a normal

ROBERT AND ELIZABETH BROWNING IN 1859

From the Talfourd Portraits

boy. He teased his father for a pony and diplomatically asked his mother not to "discourage" his father in the purchase. The pony was bought even though it entailed the necessity of a second manservant, and finances were none too flourishing. Tied to the carriage it made the journey to Rome successfully. For no longer could Elizabeth's health permit remaining in Florence in summer because of heat or in winter because of chill winds. She had been desperately ill with lung trouble which only a Gargantuan blister had — presumably — relieved. And as a consequence her beloved Florence became for her only a resting place between journeys from Siena to Rome.

Her health was once more definitely frail, partly because of her time of life, partly because of emotional shocks. Mr. Kenyon's death had been grief enough; the tactless letters which assumed that her grief would be tempered by his legacy offended her to the point of tears. And the following spring her father died, unforgiving to the last. Kindly relatives had done their best to reconcile him to his daughters. He declared that his daughters had "disgraced his family," and though he could forgive them he would not see them.

Elizabeth thought that she recognized the finality of his decision; actually she never ceased believing that he would in time relent. When after a short illness Mr. Barrett died suddenly during the night, all hope was definitely ended. When the news reached her Elizabeth collapsed.

For here again, as in her brother's drowning, she had,

she thought, much to reproach herself with. From Edward she had parted in unfriendly fashion; from her father she had parted in deception. She could not forget the months when she, planning to marry Browning without his knowledge, had used her wits to keep him unsuspecting. He had brought her flowers which she had neglected for Browning's flowers.

Oh, she had not treated him fairly. Her mind went back to her childhood when she had adored him and he had constantly indulged her. She had not been idly flattering in the dedications of her poems to him; he had been her inspiration, her audience, her public, her most encouraging critic. He had set her feet in the path she had been proud to tread all her life. He had even given her Browning; for Browning would not have been attracted to her except for her poetic gift, a gift practically implanted by her father. She owed him much, this father whom she had deceived and whom she had left without any real regret. She had not thought of his loneliness, but of her own happiness. She had written to him, to be sure; but she had never gone to Wimpole Street during her London visits to prostrate herself at his feet and honestly beg his pardon for disobedience and deception. How could she when that disobedience and deception had led to life and love ? She was his child as Penini was hers. And now she would never be forgiven. He would never see Penini, a child who would have gratified his pride far more than she had ever done.

As always in an emotional crisis Elizabeth ceased to struggle with life, giving herself up entirely to grief.

She was completely prostrated, utterly unable to cope with daily routine. At first she could not weep; after a few days tears came and for a time she did nothing but cry. Naturally her health suffered until once more she was confined to bed. There she would willingly have stayed, having no desire to stir or speak, merely the instinct to luxuriate in grief.

And then she could not restrain bitter thoughts against her father for his unreasonableness. He could have made her and surely himself happy by forgiving her. He might have had Browning's affection and Penini's. He had made her life unnatural; he had, in a way, made her a burden to her husband because of her abnormal relationships to her family. He had been even more unkind to Henrietta who needed financial assistance he could well have afforded to give, while she, Elizabeth, was without any great need. A rich man, he had not cared to smooth the path for his daughters. He had been unjust. And then would come the thought that in harboring such feelings about her father she was insulting his memory. And thus she vacillated between self-reproach and anger.

Had it not been for her husband's troubled manner, his gentle attention, his anxious solicitude she might have sunk back into her old invalidism. There was Penini, too, over-sympathetic and worried. She could not be unfair to these two who loved her. With an effort she forced herself out of the slough of pathological emotion and gradually resumed a normal life, going for short drives, and supervising Penini's lessons. She began to pick up her neglected correspondence and to take an active interest in the world. But she was definitely less strong than she had been, and she never fully regained lost ground.

She never revisited England, and indeed, made but one more excursion from Italy when in the summer of 1858 she and her family visited Browning's father and sister in France. She enjoyed travelling — though not by sea — finding it restful to be away from the possibility of unpleasant visitors, of unwanted letters, of bad news by letter or telegraph. She had not yet recovered her emotional balance, and soon she was to see her sister Arabel for the first time since her father's death. Even so she regained composure after Paris and Le Havre where she watched her husband and son swim and finally yielded to their demands that she dip into the salt water herself.

At least she had not profited by her father's death. She and her husband had in the past discussed the matter of inheritance; Mr. Barrett in spite of his attitude toward her might in view of his wealth remember her in his will. He was in many ways a just man; he certainly was a religious man. He might conceivably divide his property among all his children or such of it as was not necessarily left to the oldest son. In that case, they decided, they would not accept. They could not profit by the death of a man who had shown himself consistently inimical to them. Thanks to Mr. Kenyon who truly loved them they had plenty for their modest wants. They would be firm in refusing a legacy. But there was no legacy. When Elizabeth left her father's house she ceased to be among his children. She counted for less in his mind than a servant who had been faithful. And though she argued with herself she could not escape the knowledge that she had in reality been nothing to him. She had once been his favorite child; she had been his very darling; at least she had seemed to be. Actually she had been nothing to him. He had not cared.

From this time on a new note of cynicism crept into her letters. And the bitterness she could not control made its way into her poems.

CHAPTER XI

A S ELIZABETH'S STRENGTH waned, her physical tiredness made the world seem less bright.

> In this low world, where great Deeds die,
> What matter if we live?

she wrote in her disappointment over Italy. Here in Italy she had won her happiness and her freedom; round the very name of Italy there was for her a halo because of all it had meant to her, changing her from bedridden, father-dominated weakling to proud wife and mother, citizen of the world. It was this association of ideas that made Italy's struggle for freedom vital to her. In her personal life England had been a land of suppression; to her it now symbolized oppression. England had ignobly refused to help Italy throw off the yoke of Austria; Napoleon had nobly come to the rescue. To Napoleon her heart overflowed with gratitude; from England her heart turned with scorn.

She had never been happy in England since her marriage. Her visits there had been unsuccessful physically; and partly because of ill health, partly because of the emotional strain put upon her through her father's persistent refusal to see her, England damped her spirits. She was inclined to rationalize her personal reasons for disliking England into political reasons. The Victorian mind was distinctly patriotic and military. The righteousness of war had not yet been questioned. Italy was at war with her powerful oppressor; to Elizabeth the noble duty of England was to rush to Italy's defence. *Dulce et decorum est* was the ruling motto; the slogan "He kept us out of war" would have been a reproach, not a compliment. In this spirit Elizabeth felt actually ashamed of her country for not spilling English blood in the cause of Italian freedom.

Her *Songs Before Congress* published in 1860 expressed her disappointment over England's lassitude, Italy's mistakes, and her own infinite weariness.

She had not expected the poems to be popular in England yet she was unprepared for the unkindness of critics. Chorley, who for years the Brownings had counted among their true friends, printed a review condemning her poem *A Curse for a Nation* assuming it to be directed against England, a mistake he could not have made had he read the poem through with even cursory attention. The poem was directed to the United States then on the eve of the Civil War. Elizabeth had always been interested in America where her own poems had sold widely and where her husband's poems were loved long before England paid the slightest attention to them. She had many correspondents in America; and among the friends who visited her in Florence she counted several Americans. The American situation, then, was more than mere hearsay; she was concerned in a struggle in the home of close friends. She had rejoiced in the freeing of Jamaican slaves in spite of its effect upon her father's purse; she was troubled over the slaves in America. Her heart had ever thrilled to the word *Liberty*. Chorley, however, wrathy over the volume's preface and over the poetical reproaches to England for non-intervention in Italy, seized upon the poem as an unwarranted feminine outburst; and without reading it carefully, proceeded to flay its author.

Elizabeth's passionate partisanships had constantly laid her open to criticism. She was carried through life on waves of enthusiasm, each enthusiasm completely engulfing her. Because she never completely lost her balance in her absorption in the enthusiasm of the moment, because she made of it a living thing to which one might reasonably give one's allegiance, because her emotions, however exaggerated, were essentially sincere, she at no time appeared absurd or lightly rooted. One might or might not share her beliefs; onc usually believed in the sincerity and the beauty of Elizabeth Barrett Browning. When she bubbled over with her latest enthusiasm, one usually felt not that her beliefs were wrong, but that the world was wrong in not gibing with them.

Chorley would not have erred had he at that time been in direct personal contact with her. His ungenerous and perhaps wilfully misunderstanding criticism of the new poem deprived Elizabeth of her pleasure in the volume's ready sale and the demand for a second edition.

She was easily saddened these days. She had less resiliency under life's blows. When she needed all possible cheerfulness to offset her declining health there came news of her sister Henrietta's illness. Henrietta was dying painfully, Henrietta whose life had been full of disappointments and delays. Poverty for her in England had been far less picturesque than the Brownings' in Italy, and her sentimental captain could hardly have equalled Browning's devotion. Henrietta, moreover, had three children all younger than Penini.

What oppressed Elizabeth even more than the thought of Henrietta's suffering, was her own helplessness. Bitterly she reflected that here as always in her life she was entirely useless; she could not help those she loved, she could only be a burden to them. Always she had been the recipient, never the giver. She was eager to go to Henrietta. Wearily she gave up the idea; her presence would merely complicate the situation by adding to the burdens of others.

In these later years she had been left to herself altogether too much for a person inclined toward morbid introspection. Her husband's extraordinary devotion she never doubted any more than she doubted her influence upon him both as man and as poet. Intellectually as well as emotionally he was, as she knew, firmly united with her. Remaining lovers throughout the years they felt no distrust, no jealousy. For each the other was life itself; they were in many ways identical.

Nevertheless, her husband was cast in a different mould from hers. His restless nature could not share her placid acceptance of monotony. Her revolutions were of the mind and spirit; she lived busily within four walls. More alert physically and less inclined to regular writing he needed busy work to fill his hours. Having published *Men and Women* he seemed averse to composition, so averse that his sister became worried over his long poetical silence and intimated that it was his wife's duty to recall him to poetry.

Elizabeth, however, understood her husband. She felt that his present enthusiasm for sculpture was, on the whole, a wise relaxation, giving outlet for a vigorous man's energies and creative imagination. And since that added to Penini's music lessons and the long rides father and son now took together, was still not enough to keep his hours full she encouraged him to resume the busy social life he enjoyed.

She did not begrudge him the pleasure he found in dinners and parties, not even the pleasure he took in the friendship of other women. She never doubted him even when she felt most lonely, sitting by the fire with a novel until she crept early to bed.

But it became increasingly difficult to find strength or reason for rising in the morning. Physically she was undeniably growing more fragile. Her body had never been equal to the emotional strain of her sympathies; spiritualism, Italian liberty, English Laodicean policies, American slavery, all had excited and tired her. And now even her emotions seemed enfeebled.

In 1861 she seemed more tired than ever; the very illness which attacked her lacked vigor. Though she thought her husband unduly perturbed, she was not sorry to have him stay at home with her. She could not give way to gloom as she did when she was alone. She had

let slip from her something of her weariness and dis-
couragement in the poem, *My Heart and I,* but at least
she had not complained:

> Yet who complains ?   My heart and I ?
>   In this abundant earth no doubt
>   Is little room for things worn out:
> Disdain them, break them, throw them by.
>   And if before the days grew rough
>   We *once* were loved, used, — well enough
> I think, we've fared, my heart and I.

That sounded a bit morbid. She was never morbid
now even when coughs tormented her. It was not unpleasant to lie still, to be cherished by husband and son.
No one reproached her with her lassitude. Nor was she
left alone long hours, as she had been in her father's
house. Here her husband was almost uninterruptedly
by her side, seeming to take as much pleasure in his devotion as he gave her. She was glad that this illness had
overtaken her in Florence, dearest of cities, in Casa Guidi,
her true home. Soon she would be well and they would
go away before the heat became intolerable. But now it
was peaceful to lie still.

The cough was rather worse; but there was no need
for Robert to sit up all night; so much attention would
spoil her. He had never failed her, this poet-husband.
She had not deserved his love. She fell off into quiet
sleep, waking to find him bending over her solicitously.
She reached out her arms sleepily, and he held her close.
It came into her mind that she had never really told him
how much he meant to her, how truly she loved him.

When she had written her sonnets she had thought she loved him; had thought she knew what love was. Now after fifteen years she was just beginning to realize the depths of love, the absolute quality of her feeling for him. They had been two people then; now she could not think of either of them without the other. For all that she was a weakling and he a strong man, he was fully as dependent upon her as she upon him for love, the very source of their life. So she spoke and so they exchanged expressions of love beside which their passionate letters of years ago were weak. Completely absorbed in each other, they talked away the night until the thin fingers of dawn began to stretch across the sky. Conscience-stricken at letting her wake so long, Browning anxiously asked how she felt.

Her answer was a sleepy smile and the one word "Beautiful!" Her head sank on his shoulder and in a few minutes she was quietly asleep. Confident of an improvement in her health from this peaceful rest, Browning held very still, fearing by the least movement to disturb her. His mind went back over the joys of the past, forward into the happy years to come. She did not stir. After a long time he shifted gently and, brushing the tumbled curls from her forehead, felt with cool hand to see if the fever had broken. The great brow was cold. Elizabeth was dead.